CAMBRIDGE TEXTS IN
HISTORY OF PHILOSOPHY

D1235854

AN

*The Principles of the Most Ancient
and Modern Philosophy*

CAMBRIDGE TEXTS IN THE HISTORY OF PHILOSOPHY

Series editors

KARL AMERIKS

Professor of Philosophy, University of Notre Dame

DESMOND M. CLARKE

Professor of Philosophy, University College Cork

The main objective of Cambridge Texts in the History of Philosophy is to expand the range, variety and quality of texts in the history of philosophy which are available in English. The series includes texts by familiar names (such as Descartes and Kant) and also by less well-known authors. Wherever possible, texts are published in complete and unabridged form, and translations are specially commissioned for the series. Each volume contains a critical introduction together with a guide to further reading and any necessary glossaries and textual apparatus. The volumes are designed for student use at undergraduate and postgraduate level and will be of interest, not only to students of philosophy, but also to a wider audience of readers in the history of science, the history of theology and the history of ideas.

For a list of titles published in the series, please see end of book.

ANNE CONWAY

The Principles of the Most Ancient and Modern Philosophy

TRANSLATED AND EDITED BY

ALLISON P. COUDERT
Arizona State University

TAYLOR CORSE
Arizona State University

CAMBRIDGE
UNIVERSITY PRESS

PUBLISHED BY THE PRESS SYNDICATE OF THE UNIVERSITY OF CAMBRIDGE
The Pitt Building, Trumpington Street, Cambridge, United Kingdom

CAMBRIDGE UNIVERSITY PRESS
The Edinburgh Building, Cambridge CB2 2RU, UK   http://www.cup.cam.ac.uk
40 West 20th Street, New York, NY 10011–4211, USA   http://www.cup.org
10 Stamford Road, Oakleigh, Melbourne 3166, Australia
Ruiz de Alarcón 13, 28014 Madrid, Spain

First published 1996
Reprinted 1999

A catalogue record for this book is available from the British Library

Library of Congress Cataloguing in Publication data
Conway, Anne, 1631–1679.
The principles of the most ancient and modern philosophy/
Anne Conway; edited by Allison P. Coudert, Taylor Corse.
p.   cm. – (Cambridge texts in the history of philosophy)
Includes bibliographical references and index.
1. Philosophy. 2. Theology.
1. Coudert, Allison, 1941–   . II. Corse, Taylor, 1951–
III. Title. IV. Series.
BI201.C553P7416   1996
192–dc20   95-14825 CIP

ISBN 0 521 47335 7 hardback
ISBN 0 521 47904 5 paperback

Transferred to digital printing 2003

CE

Contents

Acknowledgments

We owe especial thanks to our editor, Desmond M. Clarke. Were it not for his conviction that Lady Conway's book merited inclusion in the Cambridge Texts in the History of Philosophy, this book would never have been published. His editorial skills have also added immeasurably to the accuracy and readability of our translation, introduction, and notes. We are also grateful to Sarah Hutton for her comments and suggestions. Last, but certainly not least, our thanks go to Joanna West, Ann Martin, Lindeth Vasey, and all those at Cambridge University Press who have turned a computer disk into a tangible book.

To Michelle and Gordon

Introduction

Anne Conway was a extraordinary figure in a remarkable age. She was all the more extraordinary because of her achievements as a woman living during an intensely patriarchal century, when women's opportunities were severely restricted and their roles limited to that of wife and mother. Anne Conway's accomplishments as a student of philosophy and theology, her mastery of the intricate doctrines of the Lurianic Kabbalah, and her authorship of a treatise criticizing Descartes, Hobbes, and Spinoza wildly exceeded the capacities of all but a tiny fraction of her female contemporaries. Her radical, indeed scandalous, conversion to the despised sect of Quakers further revealed an independence of mind wholly unexpected (and unwanted) in women at the time.[1]

Anne Finch (Lady Conway's maiden name) was born into one distinguished family and married into another. Her father, Sir Heneage Finch, had a distinguished political career as Sergeant-at-Law, Recorder of the City of London, and Speaker of the House of Commons. He died a week before Anne's birth on 14 December 1631, leaving her mother (his second wife), Elizabeth Cradock Bennett, twice widowed, with nine stepchildren in addition to her own offspring. The eldest of Anne's stepbrothers, also named Heneage, followed in his father's footsteps and was appointed to the high political offices of Solicitor General, Attorney General, Lord Keeper of the Great Seal, and Lord High Chancellor. In 1681 he was created Earl of Nottingham.

As was customary for girls, Anne Finch received no formal education. She was, however, tutored at home and may have learned a smattering of Latin at this time, although it was only later that she became proficient in that language and began to study Greek and Hebrew as well. Her earliest letters reveal her broad but unchanneled intellectual interests and her voracious reading. It was

---

[1] Sarah Hutton's article on Damaris Cudworth, cited in Further Reading, offers another example of the situation faced by an independent, intelligent, intellectually inclined woman in the seventeenth century. For a general view of the position of women see S. D. Amussen, *An Ordered Society: Gender and Class in Early Modern England* (Oxford, Basil Blackwell, 1988).

this aspect of her character that attracted the Cambridge Platonist Henry More (1614–87), who became her teacher and friend. More had been the tutor of Anne's favorite stepbrother, John Finch, while he was a student at Christ's College, Cambridge, and it was probably through this relationship that he became acquainted with Anne. In 1650 the two began to correspond about the philosophy of Descartes. Anne would quite naturally have turned to More for guidance on this subject because More was one of Descartes' earliest and most enthusiastic proponents in England at the time. This did not mean, however, that More accepted Descartes' philosophy uncritically.[2] As a committed Christian, More was acutely sensitive to the dangers for religion inherent in Cartesian dualism and in Descartes' conviction that all physical interactions could be explained in purely mechanical terms as a result of matter in motion. If, as Descartes maintained, mind and body were utterly distinct and only body was extended, then where was mind or soul, and what possible function did it serve? More feared that Descartes had inadvertently left the door open for the twin threats of atheism and materialism. He did not hesitate to voice his concerns in his letters to Descartes. Their correspondence ended shortly before he took on Anne Finch as his "heroine pupil," a term he used with obvious affection and respect.[3] He was therefore in an excellent position to instruct her in the intricacies of Cartesian philosophy.

More clearly was an exceptional as well as a rigorous teacher. For example, he did not start Anne's reading of Descartes with the *Meditations* or *Discourse*, which are so popular nowadays, but with the more difficult *Principia philosophiae*.[4] The clarity and logic of Lady Conway's thinking – which is apparent in her treatise – is therefore in large part due to More's training, although, as he was the first to admit, she was endowed with a "singular Quickness and Apprehensiveness of Understanding."[5]

More's close relationship with Lady Conway continued after her marriage to Edward Conway (1623–83) on 11 February 1651. In 1652 More dedicated his *Antidote against Atheism* to her, describing her as "Virtue become visible to his outward Sight,"[6] words that indicate his devotion and admiration. In their early letters More is very much the tutor and Lady Conway the pupil; but over time the character of their relationship changed. The subject of their correspondence branched out into other areas, and as the years went by they became intellectual

---

[2] Alan Gabbey, "Philosophia Cartesiana triumphata: Henry More (1646–1671)" in T. M. Lennon, J. M. Nicholas, and J. W. Davis (eds.), *Problems of Cartesianism* (Kingston, McGill–Queen's University Press, 1982), pp. 171–250; Gabbey, "Henry More and the Limits of Mechanism" in Sarah Hutton (ed.), *Henry More (1614–1687): Tercentenary Studies* (Dordrecht, Kluwer, 1990), pp. 19–35.

[3] Marjorie H. Nicolson (ed.), *The Conway Letters*, rev. edn, with an introduction and new material by Sarah Hutton (Oxford, Clarendon Press, 1992), p. 46.

[4] We are grateful to Sarah Hutton for pointing this out.   [5] See More's preface below, p. 3.

[6] *Antidote against Atheism* (London, 1653).

equals. More was always the first to praise the acuity of Anne Conway's intellect. He claimed that he had "scarce ever met with any Person, Man or Woman, of better Natural parts than Lady Conway."[7] Their relationship lasted until her death, although it became more distant, even strained, during the last four years of her life because of the increasingly radical nature of her theological and philosophical ideas. As More himself said of her, "She was one that would not give up her Judgment entirely unto any."[8] However difficult it was for him to accept Lady Conway's intellectual independence, especially in these later years, it is to his eternal credit that he tried.

Edward Conway succeeded his father as third Viscount Conway in 1655 and took over the management of the large family estates in Ireland and England. He too had a distinguished political career, becoming Secretary of State under Charles II.[9] Anne and Edward Conway had only one child, Heneage Edward Conway, who died of smallpox in 1660 before his second birthday. After Anne's death in 1679, Edward Conway was created Earl of Conway. Although he married twice more, he died without issue and his estates were inherited by relatives who assumed the Conway name.

While Edward Conway shared his wife's philosophical interests – he too had been a pupil of Henry More, and More dedicated *The Immortality of the Soul* (1659) to him – he was hardly prepared for the intellectual and spiritual odyssey which took her from Cartesian philosophy into the folds of Quakerism via the Lurianic Kabbalah. Aristocratic women simply did not study Latin, Greek, Hebrew, and mathematics or write philosophical treatises. In fact, if they did, they were subject to the kind of ridicule Ben Jonson reserved for a female character in the *Alchemist*:

> If you but name a word touching the Hebrew,
> She falls into her fit, and will discourse
> So learnedly of genealogies,
> As you would run mad too, to hear her, Sir. (II. i)[10]

Converting to Quakerism was even worse than claiming to be an intellectual, especially for a woman in Lady Conway's position. The Quakers were despised for their political and social radicalism as well as for their religious unorthodoxy.

---

[7] Richard Ward, *The Life of Henry More* (London, J. Downing, 1710), p. 193.

[8] Ibid., p. 196.

[9] Assessments of Lord Conway as a political figure vary widely. M. A. Thomson dismissed him as "loyal but ignorant and incapable" (*The Secretaries of State, 1681–1728* [London, 1932; rpt. New York, A. M. Kelley], 1968, p. 5). R. Hutton sees him as a "crafty and ambitious Anglo-Irishman" with "intelligence and a pleasing wit" (*Charles II* [Oxford, Clarendon Press, 1989], pp. 318, 405). Quoted in Sarah Hutton's introduction to Nicolson, *Conway Letters*, p. x, note 18.

[10] Being taken for a blue stocking was just about the worst thing that could happen to a woman at the time. The cautionary figure of "Mad Madge," the Duchess of Newcastle, was there as a terrible warning to dampen the aspirations of any would-be female intellectual. She was ridiculed for publishing works dealing with philosophy and science.

That Lady Conway should have so utterly defied conventional notions of proper female behavior, while suffering from increasingly debilitating headaches, makes her story as poignant as it is fascinating.

The major source for reconstructing the life of Anne Conway is the astonishing collection of family letters discovered by Marjorie Hope Nicolson. Nicolson brought Lady Conway and the members of her circle back to life in her edition of the *Conway Letters* (1930).[11] These letters offer a vivid picture of this highly unusual woman wrestling with theological and philosophical problems engendered by the Reformation and the "new science." Henry More acted as her guide as she pondered the religious and philosophical implications of the "mechanical philosophy," as the new science came to be called, until another figure usurped his place – the mysterious, intriguing and, by all accounts, charming Francis Mercury van Helmont (1614–98).[12]

Ironically Lady Conway met van Helmont through More. On 12 October, 1670, More invited van Helmont to dine in his rooms at Christ's College. The two men had never met, but van Helmont knew More's books and regarded them highly. More returned the admiration and took an immediate liking to van Helmont. Impressed by his "very good plaine and expert humour,"[13] and knowing of his reputation in medicine, More entreated van Helmont to try out his medical skills on his good friend Lady Conway, whose headaches had baffled such eminent physicians as William Harvey, Theodore Mayerne, and Thomas Willis.

In the years before her meeting with van Helmont, Lady Conway had been subjected to excruciating medical procedures in the hope of alleviating the terrible pains that were slowly incapacitating her.[14] She had even ventured

---

[11] Fortunately, this collection has been reissued, with a new introduction and new material by Sarah Hutton.

[12] Van Helmont has been consistently dismissed as an intellectual lightweight. For a decidedly different opinion see Allison P. Coudert, *Leibniz and the Kabbalah* (Dordrecht and Boston, Kluwer, 1994) and *The Impact of the Kabbalah in the Seventeenth Century: The Life and Thought of Francis Mercury van Helmont (1614–1698)* (Leiden, E. J. Brill, forthcoming).

[13] Nicolson, *Conway Letters*, p. 323.

[14] Thomas Willis, a noted clinical physician specializing in neurological disorders and the functioning of the brain, wrote up Lady Conway's case and described the mercury cures prescribed for her condition. Mercury is, of course, a poison, which explains why Willis admits he was so "terrified" by the effects of the supposed cure that he stopped prescribing it altogether:

> We shall consider, whether Salivation for the Curing old and confirmed Headaches is to be administered. Indeed, if the pains of the Head arise from the Venereal Disease, no doubt but that evil Remedy ought to be applyed to that evil Distemper: But having tryed that kind of remedy in Headaches arising from other causes, I found not the harvest worth the pains, and I confess some examples in those kind of cases, have terrified me from that method. A certain noble Lady (whose sickness is below described) for the Curing of a cruel and continual Headach, underwent a plentiful Salivation three times, viz., the first by Mercurial Oyntment, by the counsell of Sir Theodore Mayern, and afterwards twice by taking the lately famous Powder of Charles Huis, without any help, I wish not with some detriment: for afterwards for many years, even to this day, the disease being by degrees increased, she

across the channel to France to be trepanned. Once there, however, no one dared to perform the operation, and her jugular arteries were opened instead – an equally risky operation one would imagine! More viewed van Helmont's arrival in England as providential. Not only was he reputed to be an expert alchemist who knew the secret of transmutation, but he was also thought to possess miraculous medicines. At More's request, van Helmont agreed to visit the ailing Viscountess.[15] Thus began a friendship and collaboration that lasted until her death nine years later. Although van Helmont was unable to cure her, the two became close friends and intellectual collaborators. Van Helmont spent most of the next nine years with Lady Conway at her home, Ragley Hall, in Warwickshire. Under his aegis, she began to study the Lurianic Kabbalah and, following his lead, she converted to Quakerism. During this period Lady Conway wrote the philosophical treatise translated here. Her ideas are extraordinary, not only as the record of a woman trying to understand the reason for her own intense suffering, but also because of the radically unorthodox conclusions she reached as she tried to answer the most pressing theological and philosophical questions of the day. Her small treatise offers a valiant attempt to come to terms with the problematic features of Christianity, especially in its post-Reformation forms. Her work is essentially a theodicy, an endeavor to justify God's goodness and affirm his justice on impregnable grounds.

Lady Conway lived during a period when theology, philosophy, and science were inextricably intertwined. Her critique of the philosophy of Descartes, Hobbes, and Spinoza was motivated by her intensely religious vision of a world in which all men, whatever their faith, might live together in peace and brotherhood, praying to the same benevolent God. Her theology and philosophy are therefore all of a piece, and to understand why she accepted the esoteric doctrines of the Kabbalah, why she converted to Quakerism, and why she came to the conclusion that everything in the universe was alive and capable of some degree of perception, one must first look at the religious issues that preoccupied her.

The Christian religion has many problematic features, and these became even more glaring in the early modern period as contacts with the non-Christian world increased and factionalism within Christianity escalated. The question of

suffer'd under its heavy Tyranny . . . She had endured from an oyntment of Quicksilver, a long and troublesome Salivation, so that she ran the hazard of her life. Afterwards twice a cure was attempted (though in vain) by a Flux at the Mouth from Mercurial Powder, which the noted Empiric Charles Hues [sic] ordinarily gave. (*Two Discourses*, in *The Remaining Medical Works of that Famous and Renowned Physician Dr. Thomas Willis* . . ., 1683, pp. 122, 134; quoted in Nicolson, *Conway Letters*, p. 91, note 1).

[15] Sarah Hutton discusses Lady Conway's condition and van Helmont's care of her as a physician in "Medicine and Henry More's Circle" in *Religio Medici: Medicine and Religion in Seventeenth-Century England*, ed. A. Cunningham and O. P. Grell (Amsterdam, Rodolphi, forthcoming).

what to do with the so-called "virtuous pagans,"[16] a problem that had bothered early Christians, became more pressing as people realized how little of the world's population had, or ever would have, a chance to worship Christ and achieve salvation. Earlier thinkers rejected the idea that eminent and revered classical thinkers of the likes of Pythagoras, Plato, or Aristotle could have been damned for eternity simply because they had lived before Christ's coming; but what to do with them was another matter. Dante resolved the issue by placing his beloved Virgil in Limbo. By the seventeenth century this solution seemed mean spirited. How could Christianity claim to be a universal religion relevant to all men when salvation rested on a belief in Christ, who was an enigma to the vast majority of the world's population? This was a perplexing problem for many Christians, not least of all for Lady Conway. Further problems arose from the Christian conception of God's divine attributes. How could a just and merciful God create men and then damn them for eternity when, in his omniscience, he must have known before he created them that they were bound to sin? Didn't such foreknowledge make him utterly unjust or, even worse, the author of sin? Questions like these were made even more problematic by the doctrine of predestination. For an increasing number of people, the idea that God would actually predestine individuals to damnation was incomprehensible.

There were other equally perplexing aspects of the Christian revelation. According to Genesis, creation occurred at a specific historical moment. Many of Lady Conway's contemporaries accepted Bishop Ussher's opinion that creation occurred in 4004 B.C. But, as she points out in her treatise, if God is perfect, what would make him decide to create the world at one time rather than another? Such a decision would mean that he had changed his mind, which would imply that he was mutable and imperfect. Another theological conundrum concerned the question of whether the world was finite or infinite. If God was infinitely good, would he not create as many things as possible, indeed, an infinity of things? If one were to answer, yes, there were unsettling ramifications. If there were infinite worlds, did that mean that human beings existed elsewhere in the universe? If they did, did that, in turn, mean Christ had to be crucified and resurrected more than once and in different places? These were some of the major religious issues facing Lady Conway and her contemporaries. But the so-called "new science," or "mechanical philosophy," posed equally pressing problems.

During the sixteenth and seventeenth centuries the ancient Greek doctrine of atomism became increasingly popular. The invention of the microscope gave the theory additional plausibility since men were able to observe tiny microscopic entities for the first time. This suggested that still smaller entities, or atoms, existed from which everything was composed. Advances in mathematics also

---

[16] Louis Caperan, *Le Problème du salut des Infidèles* (Toulouse, Grand Seminaire, 1934).

favored the view that matter was made up of "solid, massy, hard, impenetrable, moveable particles," to quote Sir Isaac Newton's *Optics*, for the movements of such particles were supremely amenable to mathematical analysis.[17] The great advances made in mathematics and the science of dynamics during the sixteenth and seventeenth centuries seemed to confirm the view that every action and reaction in the physical world could be explained exclusively in terms of matter and motion. This was the basic premise of the "mechanical philosophy." It was also the basic premise of Descartes' theory of matter.

Descartes' philosophy was a product of the skeptical crisis that plagued intellectuals during the Reformation and post-Reformation period. As religious sectarianism proliferated and new scientific discoveries and theories undermined the Aristotelian world view, which had been in place for over two thousand years, many people found themselves intellectually adrift in a world that no longer seemed to offer any guidelines. If Copernicus was correct and the earth was not at the center of the universe but simply one planet among others, and if Galileo's observations of sunspots, craters on the moon, and new planetary bodies were accurate, then the assumptions men had made for thousands of years about the world and their place in it were no longer valid. In the pre-Copernican, Aristotelian universe, the earth belonged to the sublunar realm of change and decay. In this realm matter and human passions had a corrupting influence, but human beings had a choice. They could follow their base, bodily instincts, living a brutal, sinful life that would lead to eternal damnation, or they could cultivate their spiritual and rational faculties and hope for everlasting life in the ethereal, unchanging heavens – the logical place for God's kingdom. In the new Copernican universe, however, the distinction between the perfect, unchanging heavens and the imperfect earth (whose very center provided the ideal location for hell) was obliterated and with it traditional Christian cosmology. The heavens now appeared to be as blemished and mutable as the earth. Where could heaven or hell possibly be in the Copernican universe?

Traditional scientific assumptions were also undermined by the Copernican theory. Aristotle's doctrine of the four elements, each with its allotted "natural" place, made little sense on an earth hurtling through space at incredible speed in defiance of common sense. Even more important, the Copernican universe undermined the relationships and correspondences that had helped to organize human experience and give human beings some sense of security in an inherently insecure world. The ancient idea that man was a microcosm reflecting the larger world, or macrocosm, was meaningless in an infinite universe of inert, passive matter. The analogies that were such a feature of traditional society (and

---

[17] *Optics, or a Treatise of the Reflections, Refractions, Inflections and Colours of Light*, 4th edn (London, 1730) in *Heritage of Western Civilisation*, ed. J. L. Beatty and O. A. Johnson, 6th edn (2 vols., Englewood Cliffs, NJ, Prentice-Hall, 1991), vol. 2, p. 54.

that appear in Shakespeare's plays, for example) lost their plausibility. Before the seventeenth century people viewed the world in terms of a hierarchy of relationships known as "the Great Chain of Being," in which everything had its allotted place and was intricately related to everything else. We, who have lost this world, must consciously study to comprehend analogies and metaphors that our ancestors took for granted. While in earlier centuries people automatically drew an analogy between God, the king, the sun, a lion, and gold because each represented the highest degree of perfection in their respective categories, we lack the framework to weave the elements of the world into the rich tapestry of correspondences characteristic of literature, art, and philosophy up to the end of the seventeenth century. The breakdown of these correspondences and the rejection of the Aristotelian world view was traumatic for many people. John Donne voiced the disillusionment of his contemporaries when he lamented a world in which the

> . . . new Philosophy cals all in doubt,
> The Element of fire is quite put out;
> The Sunne is lost, and th' earth, and no mans wit
> Can well direct him, where to looke for it.
> And freely men confesse, that this world's spent,
> When in the Planets, and the Firmament
> They seeke so many new; they see that this
> Is crumbled out againe to his Atomis.
> 'Tis all in pieces, all cohaerence gone:
> All just supply, and all Relation:
> Prince, Subject, Father, Sonne, are things forgot,
> For every man alone thinkes he hath got
> To be a Phoenix, and that there can bee
> None of that kinde, of which he is, but hee.
> This is the worlds condition now . . .[18]

Descartes' philosophy was a reaction against this new, chaotic world. This most rational of all philosophers formulated his ideas in response to a terrifying, personal skeptical crisis that prompted him to discover the basis for an indisputably "clear and distinct" philosophy.[19] Hence the radical nature of his doubt – he would not accept anything as true until he could prove it, not even his own existence. Descartes' search for "clear and distinct" ideas finally led him to his famous statement, "I think therefore I am," which became the cornerstone of his philosophy. But he would not have accepted this seemingly

[18] "An Anatomy of the World . . . The First Anniversary," 11. 205–19 in *Major Poets of the Earlier Seventeenth Century*, ed. Barbara K. Lewalski and Andrew J. Sabol (Indianapolis, Odyssey Press, 1976), p. 111.
[19] Richard H. Popkin, *The History of Scepticism from Erasmus to Spinoza*, rev. edn (Berkeley, University of California Press, 1979).

indubitable truth unless he had first thought he had discovered an infallible argument proving the existence of a perfect God; for only the existence of such a God could ensure that his conclusion was correct.

The validity of Descartes' proposed solution to the skeptical crisis and the cogency of his arguments are not at issue here. What is at issue is the way his attempt to establish philosophy on the foundation of "clear and distinct" ideas led him to an extreme form of dualism in which mind and matter are utterly distinct and incompatible. Descartes essentially banished spirit or mind from the universe, except in the case of God, angels, and man. Because he believed that man was the only one of God's creatures to possess a soul, Descartes considered animals nothing but complicated, senseless machines. In his view, they lacked perception and feeling and acted purely mechanically, much like a bellows or pipe organ. Thus, everything in the universe, aside from man, consisted entirely of inert, passive matter; and whatever movements or actions material bodies experienced were simply the result of matter in motion.

In defining matter simply as "extension," Descartes emptied the material world of all those characteristics that give it life and meaning. Color, touch, taste, and smell are simply secondary qualities which arise in human beings when their sense organs are bombarded by colorless, odorless, tasteless, and unfeeling bits of matter. Man is truly alienated in the Cartesian universe, for there is no correspondence between reality and his perceptions of that reality. These were the ideas that Lady Conway set out to refute in her treatise.

Lady Conway's critique of Cartesian philosophy

Although we cannot be sure that Lady Conway gave her treatise the title *Principia philosophiae*, it was entirely appropriate. For while her study of philosophy began with Descartes' *Principia philosophiae*, her maturity as a philosopher entailed her rejection of his philosophy in her own very different *Principia*. Lady Conway's primary objective is to prove that Cartesian dualism is an illusion. Mind and body, or spirit and matter, simply are not and cannot be two entirely different and separate entities. If they were, they could never interact as they clearly do. However, while her arguments against mind–body dualism were primarily directed against Descartes, they also had Henry More as their target. Although More was critical of Cartesian dualism for the reasons stated above, namely that it opened the door for atheism and materialism, his own system remained basically dualistic. Therefore, in Lady Conway's opinion his philosophy suffered from the same deficiencies as Cartesianism.

Lady Conway's basic point throughout her treatise is that dualism of any kind simply fails as a philosophy because it is incapable of explaining how things in the actual world function.[20] She offers many different arguments to support this basic contention, some of which are more successful than others, as the reader will see. But one argument deserves special mention because it shows both how perceptive Lady Conway was and how useful biography can be in interpreting the work of a philosopher.[21] For understandable reasons owing to her own precarious health, Lady Conway brings up the issue of pain. If mind and body were utterly separate, why, she asks, should the soul or spirit suffer so grievously from bodily pain? Why would it not simply separate itself from the body?[22]

In raising this question, Lady Conway echoed an objection made by one of Descartes' correspondents, the Palatine Princess Elizabeth, who was the grand-daughter of James I of England and eldest daughter of the unfortunate "Winter" King and Queen of Bohemia.[23] Like Lady Conway, Elizabeth belonged to the rare breed of highly intellectual women so unusual during the period. In one of her letters to Descartes she posed the same question Lady Conway was later to raise: Why, if the mind is utterly unlike the body is it so troubled and worried by physical feelings, sensations, and emotions? Descartes

[20] For an insightful discussion of Lady Conway's criticism of More's philosophy see Sarah Hutton, "Anne Conway: critique de Henry More," *Archives de Philosophie*, forthcoming.

[21] This last point is a contentious one. Many modern literary critics deny that biography has any place in the interpretation of literature, or that the author's intended meaning is important or even possible to determine. Obviously, historians would be out of work if they accepted this line of reasoning, but then so would every scholar, including literary critics! On this question see Sean Burke, *The Death and Return of the Author: Criticism and Subjectivity in Barthes, Foucault and Derrida* (Edinburgh, Edinburgh University Press, 1992) and H. L. Hix, *Morte d'Author: An Autopsy* (Philadelphia, Temple University Press, 1990).

[22] See Chapter IX, S. 2. Interestingly enough, Descartes also realized that his theory of mind–body dualism did not seem to apply in the case of pain. As an apt and enthusiastic pupil of Cartesian philosophy, Lady Conway may have based her own objection on the following passage from Descartes' *Meditations on First Philosophy*:

> Nature also teaches me, by these sensations of pain, hunger, thirst and so on, that I am not merely present in my body as a sailor is present in a ship, but that I am very closely joined and, as it were, intermingled with it, so that I and the body form a unit. If this were not so, I, who am nothing but a thinking thing, would not feel pain when the body was hurt, but would perceive the damage purely by the intellect, just as a sailor perceives by sight if anything in his ship is broken. Similarly, when the body needed food or drink, I should have an explicit understanding of the fact, instead of having confused sensations of hunger and thirst. For these sensations of hunger, thirst, pain and so on are nothing but confused modes of thinking which arise from the union and, as it were, intermingling of the mind with the body. (*The Philosophical Writings of Descartes*, trans. John Cottingham, Robert Stoothoff, and Dugald Murdoch [3 vols., Cambridge, Cambridge University Press, 1984], vol. 2, p. 56).

[23] Elizabeth's mother, James I's daughter, married Frederick, the Elector Palatine. He became embroiled in the religious and political schisms that divided the German Empire by accepting the offer of the Bohemian crown, a position and title historically reserved for the Catholic Emperor. Frederick and Elizabeth ruled for one brief winter month (hence their sobriquet, "the Winter King and Queen") before they were routed by Catholic armies. Thus began the blood bath of the Thirty Years' War (1618–48), which left large parts of the German Empire devastated and depopulated.

never answered the question. He simply advised Elizabeth to spend only a few days a year on metaphysical matters, something he certainly never suggested to any of his male correspondents who queried aspects of his philosophy.[24]

It is significant that two women raised the same objection to Cartesian dualism. (Descartes actually went so far as to deny that he needed a brain to think!)[25] It is all the more significant because this is precisely the same objection that modern feminists have raised and continue to raise against the idea that mind and body, or reason and emotion, are antithetical.[26] The tendency to consider mind and body as a dichotomy has been detrimental to women through the ages because women have constantly been associated with the body and emotion, while men have claimed for themselves the supposedly higher realm of mind or spirit.[27]

Lady Conway raises a further objection to Descartes' radical dualism. If matter and spirit are so utterly different, how could a purely spiritual God have created matter in the first place? How could a being so completely vital, active, and spiritual have created something passive, inert, and dead?

These are the major issues which Lady Conway addresses in her short but dense treatise. All her arguments have the basic purpose of showing how destructive Cartesian philosophy is for religion and morality. For, in her view, the radical separation between matter and spirit, or mind and body, at the foundation of Cartesian science and metaphysics inevitably leads to the materialism and atheism she finds in the philosophy of Hobbes and Spinoza.[28]

The entire point of Lady Conway's critique of Descartes, and indeed of any philosophy she deemed materialistic, was to provide a secure foundation for an ecumenical religion uniting Christian, Jew, Moslem, and pagan in loving worship of a merciful and benevolent God. Her treatise provides an excellent example of how difficult it was to build the foundation for such a universal and

---

[24] Albert A. Johnstone, "The Bodily Nature of the Self or What Descartes Should Have Conceded Princess Elizabeth of Bohemia" in *Giving the Body its Due*, ed. Maxine Sheets-Johnstone (Albany, State University of New York Press, 1992), pp. 16–47.

[25] "I also distinctly showed on many occasions that the mind can operate independently of the brain; for the brain cannot in any way be employed in pure understanding, but only in imagining or perceiving by the senses" (*Philosophical Writings of Descartes*, trans. Cottingham, Stoothoff, Murdoch, vol. 2, p. 248.

[26] See, for example, Alison M. Jaggar, "Love and Knowledge: Emotion in Feminist Epistemology" in *Women and Reason*, ed. Elizabeth D. Harvey and Kathleen Okruhlik (Ann Arbor, University of Michigan Press, 1992), pp. 115–42. We do not mean to suggest, however, that only women raise this objection. William James criticized Descartes on precisely this ground (*Principles of Psychology* [New York, Dover, 1950], vol. 2, p. 451). But it is a criticism that resonates with women because they have been associated for so long with emotion, while males have been associated with reason. It is therefore especially meaningful for women to undermine the dichotomy between the two.

[27] For a discussion of the effects mind–body dualism has had on women, see the essays collected in *Women and Reason*, ed. Harvey and Okruhlik.

[28] One must admit here that Lady Conway did not fully understand Spinoza, as, indeed, did few of her contemporaries; but she did understand Hobbes.

tolerant religion on Christian foundations. There were simply too many aspects of orthodox Christian dogma that stood in the way of it becoming truly ecumenical. As we have seen, these obstacles included the belief that hell was eternal; the idea that a just and merciful God would willingly damn creatures he had created fully knowing they were bound to sin; and the notion of predestination. Added to these obstacles was the doctrine of the Trinity, which Jews interpreted as a form of polytheism, and the view that creation was an historical event which produced a finite, limited world. In her attempt to exculpate God from any possible charge of harshness and injustice and thereby create an invincible theodicy, Lady Conway strayed from the path of Christian orthodoxy into the exotic terrain of the Lurianic Kabbalah. Although her treatise can be understood on its own terms, reading it with some knowledge of the esoteric philosophy of the Kabbalah undoubtedly helps. It also allows the reader to look more closely into the mind of this highly intelligent and unusual woman, who had the courage to stand up for the ideals of tolerance and equality in an age that was just barely beginning to think in these terms. In her commitment to these ideals, Lady Conway anticipated the Enlightenment. It is all the more interesting therefore to understand precisely how such progressive notions could have emerged from the mystical theology of the Kabbalah.

Lady Conway and the Lurianic Kabbalah

The Kabbalah is the commonly used term for the mystical teachings of Judaism, especially those originating after the twelfth century. The word itself means "that which is received" or "tradition," because it was thought to represent the esoteric and unwritten aspects of the divine revelation granted to Moses on Mount Sinai, while the Bible represented the exoteric, written part of the same revelation. Lady Conway derived her knowledge of the Kabbalah from van Helmont. By the time he came to England in 1670[29] van Helmont had acquired a good knowledge of Hebrew and the Kabbalah through his friendship and collaboration with Christian Knorr von Rosenroth (1636–89), one of the most accomplished Christian Kabbalists of the seventeenth century. With van Helmont's help, von Rosenroth collected and edited the texts that eventually were published in the *Kabbala Denudata* (1677, 1684), the largest collection of kabbalistic texts published in Latin up to that time. Von Rosenroth's intention in publishing the *Kabbala Denudata* was to make available to Christians major portions of the *Zohar*, or *Book of Splendor*, one of the most important and influential expositions of kabbalistic thought. From the Renaissance onwards, Christians viewed the *Zohar* in the same light as the *Hermetica*, the *Sibylline*

---

[29] He had come as an emissary for that very Elizabeth who raised the same objection to Descartes' philosophy as Lady Conway. As James I's granddaughter, Elizabeth had been promised a pension, and van Helmont had come to try to collect it for her.

Prophecies, the *Orphica*, and those other fragmentary writings known collectively as the *Prisca Theologia*, or first philosophy, and considered to be very much older than they actually were. All these sources were thought to preserve fragments of that ancient wisdom imparted orally to Moses and which had passed down from generation to generation.[30] Being Jewish and not pagan in origin, the Kabbalah was thought by many to be the purest source for the recovery of that divine wisdom. This was von Rosenroth's justification for publishing kabbalistic texts:

> In the kabbalistic writings of the Jews I hoped I would be able to discover what remains of the ancient Barbaric–Judaic philosophy ... I had no greater wish than that I might be permitted to enjoy the sun itself and its brighter light once all the clouds of obstructions and hindrances were scattered. I scarcely hoped I would be able to catch sight of this light unless I followed the traces of that river and arrived at the spring itself. I believe that I will discover this spring in these very ancient books.[31]

In their basic aim of using the Kabbalah to convert Jews, Moslems, and pagans to Christianity while uniting Christians, van Helmont and von Rosenroth employed traditional arguments used by Christians from the Renaissance onwards to defend their interest in the Kabbalah. The kabbalistic ideas they apply to this end, however, were new and came from a body of kabbalistic writings which originated during the sixteenth century among the disciples of Isaac Luria (1534–72). The Lurianic Kabbalah was predicated on the vision of a restored and perfected universe. Gershom Scholem has explained Luria's preoccupation with redemption on historical grounds, as an attempt to make religious and philosophical sense out of the Jews' traumatic expulsion from the Iberian peninsula in the late fifteenth century.[32] In Luria's thought exile became the preliminary stage in a drama of universal redemption in which all souls would eventually return home to their divine creator. Because he considered spirit and matter opposite ends of a single continuum, Luria believed that matter would eventually be restored to its essentially spiritual state by a process of restoration, known as *tikkun*. Though the process was long and arduous, each material entity was allotted repeated reincarnations (*gilgul*), during which it would slowly move up the spiritual ladder. Exile was therefore a necessary, though transitory, stage in a process which would end in universal salvation. Pain and suffering were inevitable, but as a result of human actions in the form of *tikkunim* (positive redemptive acts) every individual would eventually be

---

[30] D. P. Walker, *The Ancient Theology: Studies in Christian Platonism from the Fifteenth to the Eighteenth Centuries* (London, Duckworth, 1972).

[31] "Amica Responsio," *Kabbala Denudata*, vol. 1, 2: pp. 75–6.

[32] *Major Trends in Jewish Mysticism* (New York: Schocken Books, 1954), p. 419. Moshe Idel does not believe that Luria's theories were a response to the expulsion. He argues instead that the Lurianic Kabbalah simply developed existing kabbalistic ideas (*Kabbalah: New Perspectives* [New Haven, Yale University Press, 1988], p. 265).

purged of the "husks" or "shards" which, according to Lurianic mythology, enveloped them when they fell from heaven into earthly exile.

Luria's thought is obscure. He delighted in allegories which invited a variety of different interpretations. In describing created souls as enveloped in "husks" or "shards," Luria elaborated on an earlier kabbalistic doctrine know as "the breaking of the vessels" (*shevirat-ha-kelim*). According to this doctrine, after the creation of the primal man, *Adam Kadmon*, the ten *sefiroth* (those attributes of the hidden God such as knowledge, strength, justice, mercy, etc., which were revealed through the process of emanation) burst from his face in an undifferentiated mass. This disordered state was only temporary because creation involved the formation of finite beings with their allotted place in the divine order. It was therefore necessary to distinguish between the *sefiroth*, which, according to Luria's mythology, should have been kept apart in separate bowls. The lights of the first three *sefiroth* were contained in bowls, but the lower *sefiroth* proved too strong, and the bowls or vessels shattered.

With "the breaking of the vessels" evil entered the world as souls became sunk in matter – or, as Luria explains more poetically – the shards of the shattered vessels fell down and became the dregs of the material world, trapping sparks of divine light. These sparks were the souls in exile. The work of redemption, or restoration (*tikkun*), consisted in freeing these sparks from their exiled state and reuniting them with the divine light.

Luria's vision of a restored and perfect universe rested on his monistic philosophy, meaning that he believed the created universe was formed from one basically spiritual substance. Luria believed that everything created is alive and full of souls at different levels of spiritual awareness and development. One of Luria's disciples, Hayyim Vital, explained Luria's ideas in a treatise included in the *Kabbala Denudata*: "There is nothing in the world, not even among silent things, such as dust and stones, that does not possess a certain life, spiritual nature, a particular planet, and its perfect form in the heavens."[33] A later Kabbalist describes Luria's theory that souls rise up the ladder of creation, becoming progressively more spiritual until finally freed from the cycle of reincarnation: "And God gradually raises these [souls] from step to step. In *gilgul* he first brings them to life as stones, and from there as plants, from there as animals, and from there as pagans and slaves, and from there as Jews."[34] Luria concluded that even eating is a holy act, but only for a wise and pious man, for he could elevate souls by incorporating them into his own flesh! "He

---

[33] "De Revolutionibus Animarum," *Kabbala Denudata*, vol. 2, 2: 415: ". . . nihil in mundo est, ne quidem inter Silentia, v. gr. pulvis terrae atque lapides, cui non sit vita quaedam, & natura Spiritualis, & planeta suus atque praefectus in supernis."

[34] Josef Schlomo Delmedigo (quoted in G. Scholem, "Seleenwanderung und Sympathie der Seelen in der jüdischen Mystik," *Sonderdruck aus Eranos Jahrbuch* 24 [Leiden, E. J. Brill, 1954], p. 103): "Und Gott hebt sie allmählich von Stufe zu Stufe; zuert bringst er sie in *Gilgul* in Gestein, von dort in Pflanzen, von dort in Tiere, von dort in Heiden und Sklaven, und von dort in Israeliten."

who is a wise disciple and eats his food with proper attention is able to elevate and restore many souls which have returned. Whoever is not attentive will not only not restore any soul, but he will also be damaged by them."[35] The unusual ideas in these last two passages reappear – but in a more ecumenical fashion – in Lady Conway's treatise, providing the basis for her defense of God as the all-wise and loving Father, who created his creatures in the full knowledge that each and every one of them would eventually be redeemed: "there are transmutations of all creatures from one species to another, as from stone to earth, from earth to grass, from grass to sheep, from sheep to human flesh, from human flesh to the lowest spirits of man, and from these to the noblest spirits . . ."[36] From this passage (and many more throughout her treatise) one can see how the Lurianic concept of *tikkun* provided both the basis for Lady Conway's criticism of Descartes' definition of matter as well as for her theodicy. Matter simply cannot be mere extension because that tells us nothing whatsoever about what matter actually is; in other words, something has to be extended and Descartes declines to say what that something is.[37] Unlike Descartes and Hobbes, Lady Conway does have a clear concept of exactly what attributes define matter. These are sensitivity, knowledge, and the capacity to improve. Her definition of matter therefore contains within it the foundation for her theodicy. God is good, just, and merciful precisely because he has created matter with the innate capacity to reach perfection through its own efforts. Just as stones had the innate capacity to work their way up the ladder of creation until they became men, so men had the capacity to become angels. Lady Conway's kabbalistic philosophy therefore led her to the optimistic belief that man possessed the ability to save himself. This idea became characteristic of later Enlightenment philosophy, but at the time Lady Conway wrote, it was a relatively novel idea as well as heretical from an orthodox Christian perspective.[38] What is especially significant and important about this passage is the emphasis it places on the role creatures play in their own redemption. That human beings were entirely responsible for redeeming the fallen world is a fundamental axiom of the Lurianic Kabbalah. Moshe Idel has described the tremendous power accorded to man in kabbalistic thought: "The focus of Kabbalistic theurgy is God, not man; the latter is given unimaginable powers to be used in order to repair the divine glory or the divine image; only his initiative can improve Divinity . . . the Jew is responsible for everything, including God, since his activity is crucial for

---

[35] *Kabbala Denudata*, vol. 2, 2: 419: ". . . qui discipulus Sapientum est, cibosq; [sic] suos comedit debita attentione: elevare & restituere potest multas animas revolutas. Qui vero non attentus est, ille non tantum nihil restituit, sed damnis quoqu; [sic] afficitur ab illis." On the subject of eating as a metaphor for the *unio mystica* see Idel, *Kabbalah*, pp. 70 ff. and Louis Jacobs, "Eating as an Act of Worship in Hasidic Thought" in *Studies in Jewish Religious and Intellectual History Presented to Alexander Altmann* . . . , ed. S. Stein and R. Loewe (Tuscaloosa, University of Alabama Press, 1979), pp. 157–66.
[36] Chapter IX, S. 5.   [37] Ibid., S. 6.   [38] Ibid.

the welfare of the cosmos."[39] Idel labels the role envisaged for man by the Kabbalah as "universe maintenance activity."[40] He contrasts the kabbalistic view that God is dependent on man with the Christian concept of man's complete dependence on God. However, it was precisely this cornerstone of Christian – and especially Lutheran and Calvinist – belief that began to crumble in the latter part of the sixteenth century. In this respect the Lurianic Kabbalah joined forces with a host of other essentially optimistic philosophies and theologies that fostered a common belief in man's inherent ability to save himself and the world.

These were the heady visions that encouraged van Helmont and Lady Conway to believe the Kabbalah offered the best possible arguments against materialism and in favor of the mercy and benevolence of God. For who could deny the goodness and justice of a God who created his creatures with the full knowledge of their eventual redemption? And who could object to a God who punished only to help his creatures improve?[41]

Van Helmont could not help Lady Conway as a physician, but in introducing her to the Lurianic Kabbalah and convincing her that pain and suffering were the prerequisites of redemption, he provided her with some consolation for her own agony. As she wrote:

> ... all pain and torment stimulates the life or spirit existing in everything which suffers. As we see from constant experience and as reason teaches us, this must necessarily happen because through pain and suffering whatever grossness or crassness is contracted by the spirit or body is diminished; and so the spirit imprisoned in such grossness or crassness is set free and becomes more spiritual and, consequently, more active and effective through pain.[42]

Lady Conway and the Quakers

Nothing might seem more incompatible than the Lurianic Kabbalah and the Quakers; for while the Lurianic Kabbalah is subtle, immensely complex, mystical, and metaphorical, the Quakers emphasized simplicity, directness, and plainness of speech. Yet at the very time that Lady Conway was deeply involved in the study of the Lurianic Kabbalah, a constant stream of Quakers visited Ragley Hall.

It is difficult to imagine now how feared and hated the Quakers were in the early years of their existence. Founded by George Fox in the 1650s, the Quakers were not originally the prosperous, respectable merchants they became in the nineteenth century. They began as conscientious objectors railing against the mainstream religions of the time as spiritually dead and overly doctrinal. The Quakers wanted to put passion and feeling back into religion. Theirs was a

[39] *Kabbalah*, p. 179.　[40] Ibid., p. 170.　[41] Chapter VII, S. 1.　[42] Ibid.

religion of the heart, a religion centered on love, universal brotherhood, and peace. And yet, to further their aims – and with the unassailable conviction that their aims, as well as their interpretation of Scripture, were divinely inspired – they routinely offended the sensibilities of the vast majority of people, who despised them and rejected their views. They would interrupt ministers in the midst of Church services, excoriating them both for what they taught and for how they taught it. The Quakers strenuously objected to the hierarchical division between clergy and congregation characteristic of most Christian denominations. During Quaker services, everyone was free to speak; even women had the right to preach, a scandalous and alarming prospect for conventional Christians brought up on St. Paul's injunction that women should be silent and certainly not teach. Quakers further enraged their contemporaries by refusing to perform duties expected of a citizen: they would not take oaths, serve in the military, or pay tithes.

For the Quakers religion was more than a set of beliefs; it involved the practical application of these beliefs. They therefore practiced what they preached to a degree that infuriated and mystified their contemporaries. For example, because they believed in the universal brotherhood of mankind, they treated all men equally, an astonishing thing to do in the intensely class-conscious, hierarchical seventeenth century. The famous (or infamous) "hat controversy" arose in this context, and van Helmont became involved in it.

Exactly when and to whom one removed one's hat was a matter of great concern and precise etiquette in the seventeenth century because it was a clear indication of personal status. By refusing to observe such formalities, the Quakers were perceived as a threat to the social order and stability. This may seem an excessive reaction to us now, but not at the time. The lines from John Donne quoted above reveal the very real fear of social chaos characteristic of the time. Donne was alarmed by precisely the kind of change in social relationships advocated by the Quakers. For Donne, relationships such as those between ruler and subject, parent and child, master and servant, and husband and wife had to be hierarchical in order to create the reciprocal bonds that preserved society from anarchy. The individualism and equality inherent in Quakerism was in no way positive; on the contrary, both promoted the social anarchy Donne saw as increasingly characteristic of a world in which every person had to be a "Phoenix," in other words, concerned solely with his own interests. Thus the "hat controversy" involved far more than hats. It was indicative of the profound change in social relationships that accompanied the transition from a feudal society, where power and position were based on birth and rank, to a competitive, capitalistic society which allowed much greater freedom and independence to the individual.

When van Helmont's close friend, Gottfried Wilhelm Leibniz, heard that van Helmont followed Quaker practice and declined to remove his hat in front of social superiors, he refused to believe it on the grounds that van Helmont was too "reasonable" to engage in such anti-social behavior:

> As for M. Helmont, I am told that he is entirely Quakerized, and that he does not bare his head when he speaks to princes. I have a hard time believing this because when I used to speak to him fairly often and familiarly eight years ago, he seemed to me entirely reasonable and since then I have esteemed him highly... [43]

Leibniz's skeptical reaction indicates how closely tied together reason, good sense, and social conformity were at the time. The Quakers outraged their contemporaries precisely because they defied social conventions. In an age when masking one's feelings and dissembling had become an art, the confrontational attitude and uncompromising behavior of the Quakers were bound to cause friction. Indeed, because they defied convention, they were labeled rabble-rousers and, even worse, "enthusiasts," a pejorative term at the time for any individual or group considered irrational and dangerous.

We who are in many respects children of the Enlightenment can appreciate the positive aspects of Quakerism and identify the ways in which Quaker teachings foreshadowed the Enlightenment ideals of liberty, equality, and fraternity. It is all the more astonishing that an English Viscountess and Flemish Baron[44] should have been able to do the same.

Of all the Quakers who came to Ragley Hall (and there were many, including the founder, George Fox, and two of its most highly educated and vocal advocates, Robert Barclay and William Penn), George Keith had the most direct effect on Lady Conway's conversion. Keith came to Ragley Hall in November 1675 in place of Penn, who was pleading in Parliament for the release of Quaker prisoners. Keith arrived as one of the leading Quaker apologists. He left, however, as a Quaker with kabbalistic leanings; and he left behind two Kabbalists with Quaker sympathies. Keith found in the Kabbalah the same answers to the same questions that bothered Lady Conway. How could Christianity be a universal religion if to be Christian and to attain salvation required a belief in the historical figure of Jesus Christ? The Quakers as a group had clearly been worried by this question. Like many of the more radical sects of the period, they emphasized an individual's immediate experience of God more than book learning. Having a sense of "Christ within" was, in their view, far more indicative of true Christian piety than the most exact knowledge of Scripture.

Keith had taken this position in the first edition of his *Immediate Revelation* (1663), written years before he visited Ragley and became acquainted with

---

[43] *Gottfried Wilhelm Leibniz: Sämtliche Schriften und Briefe*, Deutsche Akademie der Wissenschaften (Darmstadt and Berlin, Akademie-Verlag, 1923–), vol. 1, 3, p. 260.

[44] Van Helmont had been granted a patent of nobility in 1658 by Leopold, Emperor of the Holy Roman Empire, in recognition for his services to the Empire.

kabbalistic doctrine. In this book he argued that historical knowledge of Christ was not an essential aspect of Christian belief or behavior since some people have been true Christians without having heard of Christ, while others who have heard of Christ have not been Christians at all.[45] The Quakers as a whole shared Keith's concern. They continually debated which was more important, "historical" faith or "living" and "saving" faith. William Sewel, who wrote the first history of the Quakers, summarized the dilemma facing the early members:

> ... the History of the outward Coming, Nativity, Death, Resurrection and Ascension of Jesus Christ, is either necessary to Their Salvation, to whom the Scriptures came, or it is not necessary, viz. to be known and believed: If we say the Second, namely, that History is not necessary to be known and believed in order to the Salvation of us Europeans who have the Scriptures, then it will follow that we are not Christians because we deny that True, Essential, and Constitutive Character of the Christian Religion, which consists in believing that Christ was sent into the World, Born of Mary, Dead and Buried, Rose again the Third Day, Ascended into Heaven ... But if he say the First, viz. that the Knowledge and Faith of the History are necessary to our Salvation, then it will follow, that the Scripture, and not the inward Revelation of the Holy Spirit, is the Principal Rule and Foundation of that History, Faith and Knowledge.[46]

Keith helped Robert Barclay formulate the Quaker position on this issue. Writing with the approval of the sect as a whole, Keith and Barclay reaffirmed the Quakers' belief in the prime importance of the "inward" Christ; but at the same time they tried to show that they did place a Christian emphasis on the Scriptures. It was a difficult distinction to make.[47]

Even though Keith had been instrumental in formulating this position with Barclay, it is obvious that he was glad to find that the kabbalistic doctrine of reincarnation offered an escape from its ambiguities. This doctrine allowed him both to agree wholeheartedly that a Christian must believe in the historical doctrines of Christianity and yet to retain the Quaker emphasis on saving faith,

---

[45] 2nd edn (London, 1675), p. 230.

[46] *The History of the Rise, Increase and Progress of the Christian People called Quakers* ... (London, J. Sowle, 1722), p. 530.

[47] One can see from the following passages just how difficult (ibid., p. 531):

> We affirm, that tho' the Scriptures are ordinarily and commonly a certain *Medium* or *Mean*, by way of *Material Object* or Condition, for the producing of *Historical Knowledge* and *Faith* in us, and that, commonly speaking a necessary *Mean* too, as being that without which God doth not ordinarily reveal the outward *History of God and Christ*; yet we utterly deny that in *True-Christians*, the *Scripture* or *outward History* in the *Scriptures*, is the *Principal Motive*, *Foundation*, or *Principal Rule* of that *Historical Faith*, much less of Saving Faith, to the producing of which, the Letter of the *Scripture* doth very frequently (as to many of its Acts, if not all) not concur or cooperate, either as a *material object*, or as a *necessary Condition*, which is wont commonly to be called in the Schools, *Causa sine qua non*, or a Cause or Condition without which a thing cannot be done, tho' it doth not influence the Effect.

since in time every individual would have both.[48] It is something of a paradox that Keith could thus defend the legitimacy of Quakerism as truly Christian because he had accepted the kabbalistic doctrine of reincarnation!

Keith was so excited by his discovery that the Lurianic Kabbalah corroborated his way of thinking that, to use Henry More's amusing analogy, "those notions of the Cabalists . . . [became] as sweet and pleasing to him as new milk to any kitten."[49] Keith's enthusiasm proved infectious. It convinced van Helmont and Lady Conway that in the Quakers they had at last found a group which would accept their synthesis of Christian–kabbalistic beliefs and provide a nucleus for a religious movement uniting Catholics, Protestants, Moslems, pagans, and Jews.

In Lady Conway's case, there were other, even more compelling reasons for her attraction to the Quakers. As her illness progressed, she found that the only people she could stand to have around her were Quaker women. They could speak to her suffering. They were a living example of patience and resignation in the face of great bodily discomfort – the pain, cold, hunger, and squalor of continual imprisonments and public harassment had not dampened the "refreshment" the Quakers felt "in the Lord," a phrase they repeatedly used to indicate their inner consolation in the midst of horrendous conditions. Van Helmont was also struck by their ability to withstand the intense persecution they suffered during the early years of their existence. As he wrote in his "Memoirs," "it would be a strange thing to think that men should be able to endure such great and long suffering even unto Death without Divine power to support them."[50] Nothing Lady Conway had yet tried, neither the incessant and extreme use of medicines nor her continual attempt to overpower physical pain by the sheer will of intellect, had helped her. The Quakers were her final resort, and in the exigencies of pain, she tried to emulate their joy.

During the years that Lady Conway and van Helmont moved closer to Quakerism, Henry More was increasingly excluded from their company. More's biographer Richard Ward describes the tears of anguish More shed at her conversion to a sect he believed personified enthusiasm – an anathema to him:

> Now as to the Doctor's real Trouble, under this unexpected Scene at Ragley; it . . . affected him so much at length, that he receiv'd the Account of it with Tears, and labour'd all that a Faithful Friend could do, to set her right, as to her Judgment in these Matters. He both convers'd with, and wrote to these Persons, and made Remarks . . . as particularly on Mr. Keith's *Immediate Revelation*. He wrote to Mr. Pen a very excellent Letter concerning Baptism

---

[48] This issue is fully discussed in A. Coudert, "A Quaker–Kabbalist Controversy: George Fox's Reaction to Francis Mercury van Helmont," *Journal of the Warburg and Courtauld Institutes*, 39 (1976), 171–89.

[49] Nicolson, *Conway Letters*, p. 415. [50] British Library, Sloane MS 530, "Memoirs," f. 1v.

and the Lord's Supper . . . And for their great leader (as most account of him) George Fox himself, he hath said to some; That in conversing with him, he felt himself, as it were, turned into Brass. So much did the Spirit, Crookedness, or Perverseness of that Person, move and offend his Mind . . . .

As he argued thus Occasionally with these heads of the Quakers, and exercis'd his Pen both for this Lady's, and their own Benefit; so he was not wanting in his more particular Applications to her self . . . But when he saw, that he could not sufficiently prevail, he was forced to desist; and leave that Great Person to enjoy in her Extremities the Company and the Ways that she most fancied.[51]

More's attitude towards the Quakers did soften somewhat in his later years. He never could subscribe to their singularities of dress, manner, and speech, for such idiosyncrasies smacked of sectarianism. But he came to appreciate the sincerity of some of them and even to see that their thought was not as unorthodox as he had supposed. Clearly his affection and admiration for Lady Conway was great enough for him to overcome his natural antipathy for the group as a whole. As one can see in these excerpts from a letter she wrote to More shortly before her conversion, she was a valiant and persistent advocate for the Quakers:

. . . I am of your opinion, that there are many bad people amongst them, as well as of other professions, and doe also beleeve, that their converse with you might be of good use to them, for the clearing up of their understanding, and advancing their progresse towards the best things and therefore that your Conversation with them at London might be as you expresse it charitably intended, like that of a Physitian frequenting his patients for the increase or confirmation of their health, but I must professe that my converse with them is upon a contrary account, to receive health and refreshment from them. They have been and are a suffering people and are taught from the con- solation [that] has been experimentally felt by them under their great tryals to administer comfort upon occasion to others in great distresse, and as Solomon sayes, a word in due season is like apples of gold in pictures of silver. The weight of my affliction lies so very heavy upon me, that it is incredible how very seldom I can endure anyone in my chamber, but I find them so still, and very serious, that the company of such of them as I have hitherto seene, will be acceptable to me, as long as I am capable of enjoying any; the particular acquaintance with such living examples of great patience under sundry heavy exercises, both of bodily sicknesse and other calamitys (as some of them have related to me) I find begetts a more lively fayth and uninterrupted desire of approaching to such a behaviour in like exigencyes, then the most learned and Rhetorical discourses of resignation can doe, though such also are good and profitable in their season: I should not have run into this digression, but to take from you all occasion of wonder, if you should heare that I sometimes see

---

[51] Ward, *Life of Henry More*, p. 76.

some of them, that can see nobody else, for if my condition would permit it, I should desire more of their company and the knowledge of their particular experiences being refreshing to me and I hope may be of some use . . .

Towards the end of this same letter, Lady Conway gives a spirited defense of Quaker orthodoxy. She obviously has in mind the kind of thing More (and many others) routinely said about the reputed extravagance and unorthodoxy of their beliefs:

> . . . I am not in love with the name of a Quaker nor yett with what you terme their rusticity, but their principles and practices (at least most of them) as far as I am capable to judge are Christian and Apostolical; and the most of them as farr as I can see or hear live as they preach, which makes me hope (if my presage doe not deceive me) to be better served by such in my chamber, then I have yett been by any of any other profession, but of this I shall best judge after tryal, which I am now experiencing . . . for if they prove what they seeme to be lovers of quiett and retirment, they will fitt the circumstances I am in (that cannot endure any noise) better then others. I pray God give us all a clear discerning betweene Melancholy enthusiasme and true Inspiration that we may not be imposed upon to believe a lye. The great difference of opinion in this point amongst the learned and experienced occasions much perplexity in minds less exercised, and so not well fitted for judging.[52]

In 1678 the stream of Quakers who were constantly coming to Ragley was crowned by a visit from George Fox. In the months after this visit, the few remaining months of Lady Conway's life, she became a proselytizer for the Quakers in her own right. They kept Lady Conway well informed about what was happening to them throughout England. Disturbed by their stories of persecution and imprisonment, she did everything in her power to help them. Not only did she try to make her dismayed family and friends understand her conversion, but she also entreated them to intervene on behalf of the Quakers. It is an example of Lord Conway's undiminished kindness to his wife, even after her illness and conversion to Quakerism prevented her from sharing his life, that he agreed to befriend the Quakers at her request, although he clearly loathed them, as the following letter to his wife makes evident:

> All Quaker wives whose husbands I acquainted you formerly were in prison, are at this instant in the House waiting for me because Mr. Lovell the Chancelour hath appointed this day to give me an answer about them. All the matter is, I must pay the Fees my selfe, yet I hope to have them released before night, and what service soever I can doe you I shall always do it, but I finde them to be a senseless, willful ridiculous generation of people, rather to be pittied then envyed.[53]

---

[52] Nicolson, *Conway Letters*, pp. 421–2.   [53] Ibid., pp. 443–4.

Lord Conway expressed his distaste for the Quakers in another letter written the following January: "He [Frank Parsons, a servant of the Conways] tells me that you ordr'd him to returne me thanks for my kindness to your friends in the truth. If you reckon them all so that are in that profession I assure you you have a pack of as arrant knaves to your friends as any I know."[54] In her reply, Lady Conway does not comment on her husband's hostile remarks. She simply sends him and his brother some Quaker books and hopes they will speak for her. This was her final letter to her husband, and she writes as one who has finally attained the peace which the Quakers promised would come from a sincere resignation to the will of God.[55] By the time Lord Conway's reply reached Ragley, Lady Conway was too ill to read it. After two weeks of excruciating pain, on 23 February, she died. Her secretary, Charles Coke, described the circumstances in a letter to Lord Conway: "Between 7 and 8 of the Clock at night My Lady parted this life, having her perfect understanding and senses to the last minute, giving up her Spirit very peaceable without any perceivable motion and keeping a very sweet face, her pains have held her to the last . . ."[56] Van Helmont performed his last service to her as a chemist. He preserved her body in spirits of wine so that her husband could have a final look at her before her burial. She went to her grave with the simple words "Quaker Lady" her only epitaph.

The significance of Lady Conway's treatise

Except for Carolyn Merchant's work cited in our bibliography and a few articles, Anne Conway has been unjustly and unfortunately ignored by recent historians of philosophy as well as by historians in general. Taking Marjorie Nicolson's lead, Merchant tried to stimulate interest in Lady Conway by emphasizing the historical importance of the kind of vitalistic philosophy she espoused and by suggesting that her *Principles of the Most Ancient and Modern Philosophy* is a significant philosophical text both in its own right and because of its possible influence on Leibniz.

Merchant was entirely right. Aside from being the most interesting and original philosophical treatise written by a woman in the seventeenth century, *The Principles of the Most Ancient and Modern Philosophy* is a fascinating and radical philosophical treatise that sets forth a vitalistic philosophy derived largely from the Lurianic Kabbalah. Lady Conway drew on this esoteric source as she attempted to combat the twin threats of atheism and materialism, represented in her mind by Cartesianism on the one hand and Hobbes and Spinoza on the other. As we have seen, she criticized Cartesian dualism and Hobbesian materialism on the grounds that both present an inaccurate picture of the natural world and the divine attributes. Matter cannot be passive and

---

[54] Ibid., p. 446.   [55] Ibid., pp. 448–9.   [56] Ibid, p. 451.

dead as Descartes asserted, and God could not possibly be material as materialists imply since matter is in essence spirit. Instead Lady Conway offered a philosophy of *spiritual* monism, predicated on the kabbalistic doctrines of *gigul* and *tikkun*, which envisioned the restoration of the world to its originally perfect condition before the Fall. Building on the kabbalistic and neoplatonic theory of creation through emanation, Lady Conway took the radically monist position that spirit and matter were simply two ends of a single continuum. In her view, what had begun as a spiritual emanation, and only later took on material qualities, would eventually return to its original spiritual state. Such ideas were extremely radical and offensive to the orthodox of all Christian denominations because they suggested pantheism and postulated universal salvation, a concept that had been anathematized by the Catholic Church early in its history because it undermined the orthodox notion of hell as a place of eternal torment. Thus, Lady Conway's work has philosophical implications which look forward to the more tolerant and ecumenical views of Enlightenment thinkers. The way her own suffering from increasingly debilitating headaches contributed to the development of her philosophical assessment of pain as an integral part of the process of purification adds an autobiographical element to her writing that is all too often ignored in the analysis of philosophical systems.

Lady Conway's ideas are also important because of the bearing they have on Leibniz's philosophy. Marjorie Nicolson was the first to suggest that Leibniz "drew from it [Lady Conway's treatise] some of his characteristic ideas."[57] In more recent years, Carolyn Merchant returned to this subject. She too sees a similarity between the thought of Lady Conway and Leibniz, but her argument is too cautious because she was not aware of important manuscript evidence. She argues simply for a convergence between the ideas of Conway and Leibniz, not for any direct influence. New evidence shows, however, that Lady Conway's kabbalistic philosophy, a philosophy she studied with van Helmont, exerted a formative influence in the development of Leibniz's concept of "monads" and the formulation of his theodicy.[58] As Leibniz himself said in a letter to Thomas Burnett (1697):

> My philosophical views approach somewhat closely those of the late Countess Conway, and hold a middle position between Plato and Democritus, because I hold that all things take place mechanically as Democritus and Descartes contend against the views of Henry More and his followers, and hold too, nevertheless, that everything takes place according to a living principle and according to final causes – all things are full of life and consciousness, contrary to the views of the atomists.[59]

---

[57] *Conway Letters*, p. xxvii.   [58] See Coudert, *Leibniz and the Kabbalah.*
[59] C. I. Gerhardt (ed.), *Die Philosophischen Schriften von G. W. Leibniz* (7 vols., Berlin, 1875–90; rpt. Hildesheim, Olms, 1962), vol. 3, p. 217.

Leibniz became aware of Lady Conway and her treatise through his friendship with van Helmont. Van Helmont was therefore the source of kabbalistic ideas for both thinkers. In this sense van Helmont provided Leibniz with more direct access to the Lurianic Kabbala than Lady Conway. But Leibniz read and annotated her treatise and he clearly found her ideas of great interest and compatible with his own. Therefore both van Helmont and Lady Conway provided Leibniz with access to kabbalistic ideas.[60]

Leibniz rejected Cartesian dualism just as Lady Conway did and for the same reasons. Mind and matter could not possibly be separated because interaction would then be impossible. In Leibniz's philosophy, "monads" are the basic building blocks which form the created world. Unlike atoms, monads are not inert, passive bits of matter; they are characterized instead by "force" and "perception." Furthermore, they are completely self-activating and able to develop and improve. In all these ways his concept of substance is similar to Lady Conway's. Both are vitalists, meaning that matter is not moved by external forces but is itself alive and endowed with force and activity. It has been suggested that Leibniz derived the term monad from the Renaissance philosopher Giordano Bruno (1548–1600), but it is far more likely that the term came to him from van Helmont and Lady Conway.[61]

The kabbalistic concept of *tikkun* provided the basis for Lady Conway's theodicy – her defense of God as utterly just and merciful on the grounds that every creature would eventually achieve salvation. Although Leibniz does not come right out and say that every existing thing will ultimately be redeemed, as she does, there is a clear indication that this is what he actually believed and that this belief was fostered by his exposure to the Lurianic Kabbalah. Leibniz was more cautious in stating his opinions than either Lady Conway or van Helmont because he had to be. As a public official working openly for the conciliation between Catholics and Protestants, he had to be conciliatory in presenting his opinions. Nevertheless, a close reading of his few published works and a great many more unpublished manuscripts shows that he absorbed many of the kabbalistic ideas characteristic of Lady Conway's treatise. For example, by the end of Leibniz's life matter was virtually eliminated from his system and he too accepted the idea that soul (or mind) and matter are opposite ends of a continuum. Soul represents activity, while matter is simply a term for whatever impedes or hinders this activity. Like Lady Conway, Leibniz also considered time and space relative not absolute concepts, and he incorporated the concept of infinity into his philosophical system, just as she did.[62]

Viewing Leibniz from a kabbalistic perspective suggests dimensions to his thought which have previously been overlooked. This is not to say that Lady

---

[60] The question of the relative influence of van Helmont and Lady Conway on Leibniz is discussed in Coudert, *Leibniz and the Kabbala*, ch. 2.

[61] Ibid., ch. 4.   [62] For a full discussion of these issues, see ibid.

Conway, van Helmont, or the Lurianic Kabbalah were the only or most important elements that went into the making of his mature philosophy; however an appreciation of the Kabbalah offers fruitful ways of understanding some problematic aspects of key concepts in Leibniz's philosophy, such as his monadology, his theodicy, and his discussion of free will.

In conclusion, Lady Conway's treatise is interesting and important for a number of reasons. It represents an intelligent response by a vitalist to Descartes, Hobbes, and the mechanical philosophy in general. The idea that matter is merely the passive carrier of external forces, which she strenuously rejects, was a useful concept when it came to the study of physics and dynamics, for it offered a schematic and simplified view of the way bodies interact, which could be expressed in terms of mathematical formulas. The same concept of matter was too simplistic, however, to be of much use in explaining chemical reactions or biological processes, which is why advances in these sciences were much slower in coming. The mechanical-vitalist controversy continued in the following centuries.[63] With the benefit of hindsight, it is now possible to see that in many ways Lady Conway's view of matter anticipated modern physics. In this respect, what one modern scholar has said about Leibniz is equally applicable to her:

> Leibniz saw that if the only function of matter was as a passive carrier of forces, then it had no role to play in scientific explanation. Its only role would be the metaphysical one of satisfying the prejudice that forces must inhere in something more substantial than themselves. He maintained that matter was nothing other than the receptive capacity of things, or their "passive power," as he called it. Matter just was the capacity to slow other things down, and to be accelerated rather than penetrated (capacities which ghosts and shadows lack) – in other words, inertia or mass, and solidity. So, taking also into account "active powers" such as kinetic energy, Leibniz reduced matter to a complex of forces. In this he was anticipating modern field theory, which treats material particles as concentrated fields of force – an anticipation duly recognized by its founder, the Italian mathematician Ruggiero Giuseppe Boscovitch (1711–87).[64]

Because of the similarity between Lady Conway's thought and Leibniz's, her treatise is also extremely helpful in illuminating key issues which have perplexed, and continue to perplex, Leibniz scholars. She made no secret of her allegiance to kabbalistic philosophy. He, however, did, primarily out of prudence – the Kabbalah was not looked upon favorably by most Christians,

---

[63] H. Hein, "The Endurance of the Mechanism-Vitalism Controversy," *Journal of the History of Biology*, 5 (1972), 159–88.
[64] G. MacDonald Ross, *Leibniz* (Oxford, Oxford University Press, 1984), pp. 43–4.

who disapproved of anything Jewish[65] – but also because he did not want to be taken for a mystic and hence dismissed as irrational or unintelligible. Lady Conway's treatise is therefore helpful in identifying sources for Leibniz's ideas which he himself kept hidden.

Her treatise also provides an excellent example of the debt the Enlightenment owes to the occult philosophy of the previous century. Only in recent years have scholars become increasingly aware of the important ways in which mystical and magical thinking contributed to the development of our modern secular and scientifically oriented world.[66] The Kabbalah, particularly the Lurianic Kabbalah with its optimistic faith in human nature, needs to be recognized as a factor in the emergence of these new attitudes.

Lastly, Lady Conway's book is significant as the work of a highly intelligent woman who managed to transcend many of the limitations imposed on her sex at the time. Her biography therefore provides insights into the history of women during the early modern era, while her philosophy is a compelling example of the way an individual's circumstances help to shape his or her philosophy.

---

[65] Hans Joachim Schoeps has described the Baroque period as an age of philosemitism (*Philosemitismus in Barock* [Bern and Munich, Francke Verlag, 1965], but he overlooks the very real antisemitism prevalent at the time. See M. Yardeni, *Anti-Jewish Mentalities in Early-Modern Europe* (Lanham, NY, University Press of America, 1990); F. E. Manuel, *The Broken Staff: Judaism through Christian Eyes* (Cambridge, Harvard University Press, 1992); H. Oberman, *The Roots of Anti-Semitism in the Age of Renaissance and Reformation.* trans. J. I. Porter (Philadelphia, Fortress Press, 1984).

[66] See the works of Popkin, Ross, Rossi, and Webster in the Bibliography.

Chronology

Further reading

Amussen, Susan D. *An Ordered Society: Gender and Class in Early Modern England*, Oxford, Basil Blackwell, 1988

Coudert, Allison P. *Alchemy: The Philosopher's Stone*, London, Wildwood House, 1980

"A Cambridge Platonist's Kabbalist Nightmare," *Journal of the History of Ideas*, 35 (1975), 633–52

"Henry More, the Kabbalah, and the Quakers" in R. Ashcraft, R. Kroll, P. Zagorin (eds.), *Philosophy, Science, and Religion in England (1640–1700)*, Cambridge, Cambridge University Press, 1992, pp. 31–67

"The *Kabbala Denudata*: Converting Jews or Seducing Christians?" in R. H. Popkin and G. M. Weiner (eds.), *Christian-Jews and Jewish-Christians*, Dordrecht, Kluwer, 1994, pp. 73–96

Leibniz and the Kabbalah, Dordrecht and Boston, Kluwer, 1995

Duran, J. "Anne Viscountess Conway: A Seventeenth-century Rationalist," *Hypatia: A Journal of Feminist Philosophy*, Special Issue: The History of Women in Philosophy, 4 (1989), 64–79

Frankel, Lois. "Anne Finch, Viscountess Conway" in M. E. Waite (ed.), *A History of Women Philosophers*, 3 vols., Dordrecht, Kluwer, 1991, vol. 3, pp. 41–58

Harvey, Elizabeth D. and Kathleen Okruhlik (eds.). *Women and Reason*, Ann Arbor, University of Michigan Press, 1992

Hutton, Sarah. "Anne Conway" in Robert Audi (ed.), *The Cambridge Dictionary of Philosophy*, Cambridge, Cambridge University Press, forthcoming

"Anne Conway" in E. Craig (ed.), *The Routledge Encyclopedia of Philosophy*, London, Routledge, forthcoming

"Anne Conway: critique de Henry More," *Archives de Philosophie*, forthcoming

"Between Platonism and Enlightenment: Damaris Cudworth, Lady Masham," *British Journal for the History of Philosophy*, 1 (1993), 29–54

(ed.). *Henry More (1614–1687): Tercentenary Studies*, Dordrecht, Kluwer, 1990

"Medicine and Henry More's Circle" in A. Cunningham and O. P. Grell (eds.), *Religio Medici: Medicine and Religion in Seventeenth-Century England*, Amsterdam, Rodolphi, forthcoming

Idel, Moshe. *Kabbalah: New Perspectives*, New Haven, Yale University Press, 1988

Jaggar, Alison M. "Love and Knowledge: Emotion in Feminist Epistemology" in Harvey and Okruhlik (eds.), *Women and Reason*, pp. 115–42

Johnstone, Albert A. "The Bodily Nature of the Self or What Descartes Should Have Conceded Princess Elizabeth of Bohemia" in Maxine Sheets-Johnstone (ed.), *Giving the Body its Due*, SUNY series: *The Body in Culture, History, and Religion*, ed. H. Eilberg-Schwartz. Albany, State University of New York Press, 1992, pp. 16–47

Merchant (Iltis), Carolyn. *The Death of Nature: Women, Ecology, and the Scientific Revolution*, New York, Harper & Row, 1980

"The Vitalism of Anne Conway: Its Impact on Leibniz's Concept of the Monad," *Journal of the History of Philosophy*, 17 (1979), 255–69

Mintz, S. E. *The Hunting of Leviathan: Seventeenth-century Reactions to the Materialism and Moral Philosophy of Thomas Hobbes.* Cambridge, MA, Harvard University Press, 1962

Nicolson, Marjorie H. (ed.). *The Conway Letters*, rev. edn, with an introduction and new material by Sarah Hutton, Oxford, Clarendon Press, 1992

Orio d Miguel, B. "Leibniz und 'die physischen Monaden' von Fr. M. van Helmont" in I. Marchlewitz and A. Heinekamp (eds.), *Leibniz' Auseinandersetzung mit Vorgängern und Zeitgenossen*, Studia Leibnitiana Supplementa 27, Stuttgart, Franz Steiner, 1990, pp. 147–56

Owen, Gilbert R. "The Famous Case of Lady Anne Conway," *Annals of Medical History*, 9 (1937), 567–71

Popkin, Richard H. *The History of Scepticism from Erasmus to Spinoza*, rev. edn, Berkeley, University of California Press, 1979

"The Spiritualistic Cosmologies of Henry More and Anne Conway" in Sarah Hutton (ed.), *Henry More: Tercentenary Studies*, Dordrecht, Kluwer, 1990, pp. 97–114

The Third Force in Seventeenth-Century Thought, Leiden, E. J. Brill, 1992

Ross, G. MacDonald. *Leibniz*, Oxford, Oxford University Press, 1984

"Occultism and Philosophy in the Seventeenth Century" in A. J. Holland (ed.), *Philosophy, Its History and Historiography*, Dordrecht, D. Reidel, 1985, pp. 95–115

Rossi, Paolo. *Francis Bacon: From Magic to Science*, London, Routledge & Kegan Paul, 1968

Scholem, Gershom. *Kabbalah*, New York, Meridian, 1974

Major Trends in Jewish Mysticism, New York, Schocken Books, 1954.

Watson, R. A. *The Breakdown of Cartesian Metaphysics*, Atlantic Highlands, NJ, Humanities Press International, Inc., 1987

    The Downfall of Cartesianism, 1673–1712: A Study of Epistemological Issues in Late 17th Century Cartesianism, The Hague, Marinus Nijhoff, 1966

Webster, Charles. *From Paracelsus to Newton: Magic and the Making of Modern Science*, Cambridge, Cambridge University Press, 1982

Note on the text

Anne Conway wrote *The Principles of the Most Ancient and Modern Philosophy* in English some time during the last nine years of her life. The similarity between many of her ideas and the kabbalistic philosophy of Francis Mercury van Helmont led Marjorie Hope Nicolson to conjecture that Lady Conway began to write the manuscript shortly after van Helmont came to stay with her in 1671, and that she completed it before she became involved with the Quakers in 1675, since there are no references to them. After her death in 1679, van Helmont took the treatise with him to the continent, where he intended to have it published. However, it was not published until 1690, at which time it appeared in Amsterdam in Latin as the first of three treatises in a collection entitled *Opuscula philosophica*. The collection also included a Latin translation of van Helmont's *Two Hundred Queries . . . Concerning the Doctrine of the Revolution of Souls* (1684), a treatise which Lady Conway and the Quaker George Keith had helped van Helmont write and which is similar to her work in many respects.[1] By the time Lady Conway's book was published in English in 1692 the original manuscript had apparently been lost because the translator "J. C." specifically says that he had made his translation from the Latin edition. In the *Dictionary of National Biography* "J. C." is identified as Jacobus Crull. No reason is given. Marjorie Nicolson concluded that John Clark, M.D., who translated van Helmont's *Seder Olam* in 1694, is a more likely choice.[2]

An edition comprising both the Latin version and the English translation was edited by Peter Loptson and published by Martinus Nijhoff in 1982 as part of their *International Archives of the History of Ideas*. The English translation is,

---

[1] Lady Conway also collaborated with van Helmont on his *Cabbalistical Dialogue* (London, 1682), which was first published in Latin in the *Kabbala Denudata* (Sulzbach, 1677). See Allison P. Coudert, *The Impact of the Kabbalah in the Seventeenth Century: The Life and Thought of Francis Mercury van Helmont (1614–1698)* (Leiden, E. J. Brill, 1995).

[2] Marjorie H. Nicolson (ed.), *The Conway Letters*, rev. edn, with an introduction and new material by Sarah Hutton (Oxford, Clarendon Press, 1992), p. 453.

however, virtually incomprehensible in places, not only because of the anti-quated nature of the English but also because the translator misunderstood or misinterpreted certain important aspects of Lady Conway's thought.

The translators of the present edition have tried to produce a modern translation in idiomatic English that is both true to the spirit of the Latin and an accurate reflection of Lady Conway's highly original philosophy. While her ideas are perfectly comprehensible in the context of her treatise as a whole, our introduction is intended to provide the reader with an understanding of the personal and historical circumstances that shaped her philosophy. The notes are also designed to help the reader. They are divided into two sorts. Those in the main text designated by letters were an integral part of the original Latin text. In all probability they were added by van Helmont after Lady Conway's death. These notes refer to relevant sections of the *Kabbala Denudata* (which is discussed in our introduction). Because these notes tend to interrupt the flow of Lady Conway's argument, we have decided to take them out of the text itself and place them at the bottom of the page.

In addition to the short preface that was published with the book, we have included a longer preface written by Henry More, probably shortly after Lady Conway's death. Although it was never published, it gives a vivid picture of her and the circumstances in which she wrote her book. It will also give the reader a sense of what seventeenth-century English prose, spelling, and punctuation were like. From a comment made by More's biographer, Richard Ward, it appears that More and van Helmont collaborated in the publication of Lady Conway's work, and that More actually wrote the preface, although it is signed by van Helmont. This explains why the preface sounds in places as if it were written by van Helmont, while in others as if written by More. As Ward says,

> There was a Design once (from certain Hands I could mention) of Printing some Remains of this Excellent Lady: Upon which Occasion (for wise and good Reasons, though in the Name of another Person) he [More] thought fit to write the ensuing Account, by way of Preface to the *Reader* . . .[3]

[3] Richard Ward, *The Life of Henry More* (London, J. Downing, 1710), pp. 202–3.

The Principles of the Most Ancient and Modern Philosophy concerning God, Christ and Creation, that is, concerning the Nature of Spirit and Matter, thanks to which all the Problems can be resolved which could not be resolved by Scholastic Philosophy nor by Modern Philosophy in general, whether Cartesian, Hobbesian, or Spinozian. A Short Posthumous Work translated from English into Latin, with annotations taken from the ancient philosophy of the Hebrews.

By Anne Conway.
Amsterdam, 1690.

Preface by Henry More

These Fragments of that incomparable Person, the Lady Viscountess Conway, which are put into thy Hands for thine Edification; that they may neither prove an Offense to thy self, nor an Injury to the deceas'd Author, as seeming less suitable to those singular Natural Parts and Wit that God had bestow'd upon her, besides those admirable acquir'd Accomplishments in the chiefest and Choicest Parts of Knowledge, as well Natural as Divine; Thou art to understand, that they are only Writings abruptly and scatteredly, I may add also obscurely, written in a Paper-Book, with a Black-lead Pen, towards the latter end of her long and tedious Pains and Sickness; which She never had Opportunity to revise, correct, or perfect. But so Sincere and Pious a Spirit breathing in them, it was thought Fit by some to make them Publick: It being hopeful, that these broken Fragments of so Entire and Sincere a Soul, may prove the Bread of Life to as many as have an unfeign'd Hunger after true Holiness and Righteousness. Wherefore I desire thee, that thou would'st Candidly interpret, what in Kindness is offer'd to thee; and to admire with me the Sound Judgment and Experience of this Excellent Personage: Who abounding with that which the Natural Man sets so high a Price upon (I mean, not only Nobleness of Birth, and Greatness of Quality and Fortune in the World, and extraordinary Dearness to her nearest Relations and Friends, but) that singular Quickness and Apprehensiveness of Understanding, for the enabling her to the attaining all manner of Knowledge in Arts and Sciences; besides a marvellous Sagacity and Prudence in any Affairs of Moment, wherein her Quickness and Solidness of Judgment was surprising, to as many as had Occasion and Opportunity to consult with her: I say, though abounding with these, yet nothing was so surprising to the Serious, who have known her from her Youth, as that she had so timely a Sense and Relish of what is infinitely above all these things, and accordingly esteem'd it; which is the saving Knowledge of our Lord Jesus, the Knowledge of Christ in us, (that is, of his Power, Life, and Spirit in us) the Hope of Glory.

In vertue of this chiefly, if not solely, was she enabled, with that marvellous Patience, to undergo those long and tedious Pains of her Head (which after seiz'd on her Body also) which otherwise had been plainly unsupportable to Flesh and Blood. And to the Astonishment of that Party, who knew her from her Youth, and had the Honour of her Friendship, to her dying Day; Though She was troubled with these Pains some Years before his Acquaintance with her, and they were growing upon her still more and more till, besides her High and Intolerable Fits or Paroxysms, She had continuance of Pain perpetual upon her, Such as would have prov'd unsufferable Paroxysms to others: Yet notwithstanding these great Impediments, and hard Batterie laid against her Intellectuals, her

3

Understanding continued quick and sound, and had the greatest Facility imaginable for any, either Physical, Metaphysical, or Mathematical Speculations; so that She understood perfectly, not only the true System of the World, call it Copernican or Pythgorick as you will, with all the Demonstrative Arguments thereof; but all Descartes his Philosophy, as also all the Writings of him, who (though a Friend of Descartes, yet) out of Love to the Truth, hath so openly for this good while oppos'd his Errors:[1] To say nothing of her persuing (by the Benefit of the Latin Tongue, which she acquir'd the Skill of notwithstanding these great Impediments) of both Plato and Plotinus, and of her searching into, and judiciously sifting the abstusest Writers of Theosophy; which, that party can testifie, was not out of any Vanity of Mind, or fond Curiosity, but it was, as it were, the genuine Food of her Natural Genius: Nor could he ever observe, while She could come abroad and Converse, that She would ever ostentate her Knowledge; or so much as make any Discovery of it, upon never so fair an Opportunity; According to that Saying, writ on the In-side of a Paper-Book She had had a long time by her, and upon Occasion gave that Party, and may well be added to her plain Parables; Ignorance is better than Pride.

And indeed these Christian graces, that shin'd in her all along this Close Pursuit of Truth and Knowledge, were so Eminent, that they might justly seem to obscure the Lustre of her other Accomplishments, with those that had Eyes to behold them, and were competent Judges of them. For whereas such Pains, so great, and so incurable (For they were so great, that nothing but the Intolerableness, could make her undergo such painful and coarse Remedies, worse than any Pain or Disease else could be, in any ordinary Man's Judgment; and so incurable, that they puzzled and defeated all the Attempts of all Physicians whatsoever; Galenists, Chymists, Empiricks, as well French as English; for she went into France on purpose to have her Cranium open'd (but none durst adventure on it, though they opened her Jugular Arteries) in order to the Curing of her Disease: So that at last She was fain to Cease from making any more Trials. Which was the very Advice, which that Party, her Faithful Friend[2] gave her betimes; namely to betake her self wholly to GOD, and to make that Noble Experiment, whether the Consummate Health of her Soul, would not recover also, in due time, the Health of her Body. But he confess'd withall, that it seem'd Morally impossible for any one in such Circumstances of Extremity, not to make trial of any Natural means that might give any Hope of Relief. But it seems not without a Providence, that All means prov'd so ineffectual; that the Power of God in a Regenerate Soul might the more manifestly appear, how victorious it is, even in the extremest Afflictions and Temptations. For, what I was agoing to say, whereas such Pain, so great and intolerable doth ordinarily empeevish the

---

[1] More is referring to himself.   [2] More is again referring to himself.

4

Spirit of the Afflicted, and makes their Conversation ungrateful to Others, their Minds being taken up with their own Sufferings; I can witness from these Seven or Eight Years Experience of her,[3] and that other Party,[4] whom I have so often mentioned, for Four times as long again, that her Conversation was always with that Meekness, Kindness, and Discretion, even to those that have not fairly, if not provokingly carried themselves towards her, in their pretended Friendship, that I cannot think of it without Admiration and Astonishment; and how Ready She was to put a good Sense upon Other Folks Actions, though Strangers, when their Credit hath been diminish'd by a Proud and Envious Tongue: And Lastly, how in the midst of her insupportable Pains and Afflictions, which continued upon her to the Last; and which do naturally nail down, as it were, and fix the Mind of an Ordinary Soul, to its own Personal Concerns; how yet She bore the Care, and Provident Sollicitude, for all her Friends, and of her nearest Relations the most; which she did, in a manner, to her very last Breath (as I can witness, that was present with her when she died)[5] as if She had been appointed by God the Common Good Genius, or Tutelar Angel, of all her Friends and Relations, even while She was in the Flesh. For though her Pains encreas'd, yet her Understanding diminsh'd not; and in Contradiction to that Common Aphorism, She dyed without any Fever, merely of her Pains, drawing her Breath a while as one asleep, without throatling, and with her Eyes open, and presently after giving up the Ghost. Her Antient Friend[6] being acquainted with the Circumstances of her Death from Ragley, return'd only this short Answer, "I perceive, and bless God for it, that my Lady Conway was my Lady Conway to her Last Breath; the greatest Example of Patience and Presence of Mind, in highest Extremities of Pain and Affliction, that we shall easily meet with: Scarce any thing to be found like her, since the Primitive times of the Church." Of her Supernatural Comforts and Refreshments after some of her greatest Agonies and Conflicts, and of her strange Praevisions of things future, I might here also make mention, but I hold it less necessary.

And these things which I have Communicated to thee, concerning our Friend, this Excellent Lady; I have not done it out of any Partial or Carnal Boastings: But that God may be fortified, and that thou mayst the more fully understand; That that Religion, that availth any thing in the time of Distress, is not Opinion, Ceremony, Talk, or Fancy, but the Power of God in the inward Man, in Vertue of the New Birth, or Real Regeneration, which is the true and saving Knowledge of Christ in us, the Hope of Glory. Which Mystery She being acquainted with from her Youth, and growing up therein; it made her such an invincible Champion, and enabled her to bear up with that Stoutness and Constancy, either against the Buffetings of Satan, or sad Incumbrances of

---

[3] This refers to van Helmont.   [4] More.   [5] Van Helmont.   [6] More.

Afflictive Nature; in which, by the Divine Power in the New Birth, She hath prov'd her self more than Conquerour.

To the Attaining which Blessed State, if these Papers, which I have put into thy Hands, may contribute any thing, I shall much rejoice thereat: In the mean time, I desire thee, that thou would'st accept this Office of Love from,

Thine in the Truth, as it is in Jesus

FR. MER. HELMONT

Published Preface

Kind Reader, we have published this short work for your sake, which was written a few years ago by an English Countess, a woman learned beyond her sex, most skilled in Greek and Latin literature, and especially well versed in every sort of philosophy. As soon as she was taught the principles of Descartes, having seen their faults, she later discovered so many things from reading certain writings of genuine ancient philosophy that she wrote these few chapters for her own use, but in a very small and faint handwriting. When these were found after her death, part of them were transcribed (because the rest were hardly legible) and translated into Latin, so that the whole world might derive some profit from them. These are now public property, so that anyone may admire the author and recognize true philosophy and more easily avoid these errors, which are now, alas, all too common. Enjoy these writings and farewell.

Chapter I
God and his divine attributes

Sections 1, 2, 3, 4, 5 concern God and his divine attributes. Sections 6 & 7 show how the Trinity could be conceived in God according to Scripture so that Jews, Turks, or other peoples would not be offended, if these words, "three distinct persons," which are not in Scripture and have no reasonable sense, are omitted.

S. 1. God is spirit, light, and life, infinitely wise, good, just, strong, all-knowing, all-present, all-powerful, the creator and maker of all things visible and invisible.[a]

S. 2. In God there is no time, change, arrangement, or division of parts. For he is wholly and universally one in himself and within himself without any variation or admixture. In himself he has no darkness or corporeality at all, nor any form, image, or figure whatsoever.[b]

S. 3. He is also in a true and real sense an essence or substance distinct from his creatures, although not divided or separate from them but present in everything most closely and intimately in the highest degree. Nevertheless, they are not parts of him or changeable into him, just as he is not changeable into them. He himself is also in a true and real sense the creator of all things, who not only gives to them form and figure but also essence, life, body, and whatever good they have.[c]

S. 4. And since there is no time in him nor any mutability, there can exist in him no new knowledge or will at all, but his will and knowledge are eternal and without time or beyond time.[d]

S. 5. Similarly, in God there exists none of the passions which proceed from his creatures, if we wish to speak correctly. For every passion is temporal, having its beginning and end in time.

[a] See *Adumbratio Kabbalisticae Christianae*, ch. 2, sec. 2–7, *Kabbala Denudata*, ii, last tract.
[b] See *Philosophiae Kabbalisticae Dissertatio*, ch. 3, *Kabbala Denudata*, i, pt. 3.
[c] See *Kabbala Denudata*, i, pt. 2, pp. 30, 332.
[d] See *Philosophiae Kabbalisticae Dissertatio*, 3, ch. 1, *Kabbala Denudata*, i, pt. 3, & ibid., ch. 6.

S. 6. In God there is an idea which is his image or the word existing within himself, which in substance or essence is one and the same with him, through which he knows himself as well as all other things and, indeed, all creatures were made or created according to this very idea or word.

S. 7. For the same reason there is spirit or will in God, which comes from him and which is in terms of substance or essence nevertheless one with him, through which creatures receive their essence and activity; for creatures have their essence and existence purely from him because God, whose will agrees with his most infinite knowledge, wishes them to exist. And thus wisdom and will in God are not entities or substances distinct from him but, in fact, distinct modes or properties of one and the same substance. And this is that very thing which those who are the most knowledgeable and judicious among Christians understand by the Trinity. If the phrase concerning the three distinct persons were omitted – for it is a stumbling block and offense to Jews, Turks, and other people, has truly no reasonable sense in itself, and is found nowhere in Scripture – then all could easily agree on this article. For they hardly deny that God has wisdom, an essential idea, and such a word in himself by which he knows all things. And when they concede that the same being gives essence to all things, they are forced by necessity to acknowledge that the will exists in him through which he maintains and brings into actual being that which was hidden in the idea, so that he produces and makes a distinct and essential substance. And this is surely to create the essence of a creature, for the idea alone does not confer being on a creature, but only will conjoined with the idea, just as an architect may have an idea of a house in his mind, yet the idea alone does not build the house, but will is joined with it and cooperates with it.

Annotations to the First Chapter

The ancient hypothesis of the Hebrews in respect to the last part of this chapter is as follows:

1. Since God was the most intense and infinite light of all things as well as the supreme good, he wished to create living beings with whom he could communicate. But they could in no way endure the very great intensity of his light. These words of Scripture apply to this: "God dwells in inaccessible light. No one has ever seen him, etc." (1 Timothy 6:16).[1]

2. For the sake of his creatures (so that there might be a place for them) he diminished the highest degree of his intense light. Thus a place arose, like an empty circle, a space for worlds.

3. This void was not privation or non-being but an actual place of diminished light, which was the soul of the Messiah, called *Adam Kadmon* by the Hebrews, who filled this entire space.

[1] Although Lady Conway does not provide biblical references, the editors thought it useful to do so.

4. This soul of the Messiah was united with the entire divine light, which remained in the void to a lesser degree, so that it could be tolerated. This soul and light constituted one entity.

5. This Messiah (called *logos* or the word and the first-born son of God) made from within himself (the diminution of his light having recently occurred for the convenience of the creatures) the succession of all creatures.

6. The light of his divine nature was shared with them as objects of his contemplation and love. These were the forces uniting the creator and his creatures, in which union their happiness lay.

7. This is the reason why the Trinity represents God. The first concept is the infinite God himself, considered above and beyond his creation; the second is the same God insofar as he is the Messiah; the third is the same God insofar as he is with the Messiah in creatures, with the lowest degree of light which is adapted to the perception of creatures. That saying of Scripture (John 1:18) pertains to this: "No one has ever seen God" (this refers to the first concept); "the son who is in the bosom of the Father" (this refers to the second concept); "has revealed him [God] to us" (this refers to the third member of the Trinity).

8. But it is customary among the Hebrews to use the word "person" in this way, so that it does not mean to them an individual substance but merely a concept for representing a species or for considering a mode.[e]

---

[e] See *Adumbratio Kabbalisticae Christianae*, ch. 2 & 3.

Chapter II

S. 1. Creatures, although they are not coeternal with God, nevertheless have existed for an infinite time from the beginning. S. 2. Thus, no number of years, not even the greatest that the created intellect could imagine, can arrive at the beginning of their creation. S. 3. In different senses, creatures have existed and not existed from eternity. S. 4. The infinity of time is confirmed by the infinite goodness of God. S. 5. The essential attribute of God is to be the creator. S. 6. What is time and why it is not in God.

S. 1. All creatures simply are and exist only because God wishes them to, since his will is infinitely powerful and his command, without any help, instrumental cause, or matter, is alone capable of giving existence to creatures. Hence, since the will of God is eternal or from eternity, it follows necessarily that creation results immediately, and without any interval of time, from the will to create. And yet it cannot be said that creatures considered in themselves are coeternal with God because then eternity and time would be confused with each other. Nevertheless, creatures and the will which created them are so mutually present and happen one after another so immediately that nothing can intervene, just as if two circles should immediately touch each other. Nor can we assign to creatures any other beginning than God himself and his eternal will, which agrees with his eternal idea or wisdom. The natural consequence of this is that time is infinite from the moment of creation and has no quantity which the created intellect can conceive. For in what way could it be finite or measured since it has no other beginning than eternity itself?

S. 2. But if someone should say that time is finite, let us suppose that there were about six thousand years from the beginning (some people think the length of time could hardly be longer). Or let us suppose with others (who think that before this world there was another invisible world and the visible world came from this) that the duration of the world was six hundred thousand years, or some other number as great as possible, which can in no way be conceived of. I ask if the world could have been created earlier or before this time? If they deny this, they restrict the power of God to a certain number of years. But if they affirm this, they admit that there was time before all times, which is a manifest contradiction.

S. 3. With these things established, one may easily answer the question which has greatly worried so many people, namely, whether creation occurred or could have occurred from eternity or from the beginning of time. For, if they understand by eternity and by time everlasting an infinite number of times, then, in this sense, creation was made from the beginning of time. If, however, they mean such eternity as God has – so that it must be said that creatures are coeternal with God and lack a beginning – this is false. For creatures, like times, which are nothing but successive motions and operations of creatures, have a beginning, which is God or the eternal will of God. And why should anyone wonder if times, taken as a whole and universally, are called infinite, since it is possible to conceive that even the least amount of time has in itself the appearance of infinity? For just as no time is so great that it is not possible to conceive of a greater, so likewise no time is so small that a lesser may not be imagined, for a sixtieth part of a minute may be divided into sixty other parts and these into still others, and so on to infinity.

S. 4. The infinity of time from the beginning of creation can likewise be proved by the goodness of God. For God is infinitely good, loving, and bountiful; indeed, he is goodness and charity itself, the infinite fountain and ocean of goodness, charity, and bounty. In what way is it possible for that fountain not to flow perpetually and to send forth living waters? For will not that ocean overflow in its perpetual emanation and continual flux for the production of creatures? For the goodness of God is communicated and multiplied by its own nature, since in himself he lacks nothing nor can anything be added to him because of his absolute fullness and his remarkable and mighty abundance. And since he is not able to multiply himself because that would be the same as creating many Gods, which would be a contradiction, it necessarily follows that he gave being to creatures from time everlasting or from time without number, for otherwise the goodness communicated by God, which is his essential attribute, would indeed be finite and could be then numbered in terms of years. Nothing is more absurd.

S. 5. Therefore the essential attribute of God is to be the creator. Consequently God was always a creator and will always be a creator because otherwise he would change. Therefore creatures always were and always will be. Moreover, the eternity of creatures is nothing other than an infinity of times in which they were and always will be without end. Nevertheless, this infinity of time is not equal to the infinite eternity of God since the divine eternity has no times in it and nothing in it can be said to be past or future, but it is always and

13

wholly present. And while he is in time, he is not bound by time. Although the Hebrews speak a little differently about these matters,[f] nevertheless they do not contradict this opinion since they allow an indefinite duration of time.[g]

S. 6. And the reason for this is obvious because time is nothing but the successive motion or operation of creatures, and if this motion or operation should cease, then time itself would cease and the creatures themselves would end with time since the nature of every creature is to be in motion or to have motion, by which means it progresses and grows to its ultimate perfection. And since in God there is no successive motion or operation toward further perfection because he is absolutely perfect, there are no times in God or his eternity. Furthermore, because there are no parts in God, there are also no times in him since all times have parts and are divisible into infinity, as already said.

[f] As appears in the *Kabbala Denudata*, i, pt. 2, pp. 29–30, and in *Philosophiae Kabbalisticae Dissertatio*, ch. 6 & 7, *Kabbala Denudata*, i, pt. 3.

[g] *Adumbratio Kabbalae Christianae*, ch. 7. sec. 4, 5, 7; *Kabbala Denudata*, ii, last tract.

Chapter III

S. 1. God is a most free agent and yet most necessary. S. 2. The indifference of the will, which the Scholastics believe is in God, is pure fiction. S. 3. God created the world not because of some external necessity but from the inner impulse of his divine goodness and wisdom. S. 4. There are infinite creatures and infinite created worlds. S. 5. The smallest creature of which we can conceive has infinite creatures in itself. S. 6. This, however, does not make them equal to God. S. 7. A refutation of imaginary spaces which were invented by the Scholastics as if they existed apart from creatures. S. 8. Successive motion has no place in God. S. 9. An answer to the objection. S. 10. All creatures are united in a certain way.

S. 1. Moreover, if the aforementioned attributes of God are duly considered, and especially these two, namely his wisdom and goodness, then it is possible utterly to refute and eliminate that indifference of the will which the Scholastics and those falsely called Philosophers believe to be in God and which they incorrectly call free will. For although the will of God is most free so that whatever he does in regard to his creatures is done without any external force or compulsion or without any cause coming from the creatures (since he is free and acts spontaneously in whatever he does), nevertheless, that indifference of acting or not acting can in no way be said to be in God, for this would be an imperfection and would make God like his corruptible creatures. For this indifference of will is the basis for all mutability and corruptibility in creatures, so that there would be no evil in creatures if they were not mutable. If the same indifference of will were predicated of God, he would be assumed to be mutable and consequently would become like corruptible man, who often acts from pure will but without any true and solid reason or the guidance of wisdom. Thus, he would be like those cruel tyrants in the world who do most things from their own pure will, relying on their power, so that they are unable to give any explanation for their actions other than their own pure will. Yet, since any good man is able to give a suitable explanation for what he does or will do because he understands that true goodness and wisdom require that he do so, he therefore wishes to act as he does because it is right and knows that if he does not, he will neglect his duty.

S. 2. Therefore true justice or goodness has no latitude or indifference in itself but is like a straight line drawn from one point to another, where it is impossible to have two or more equally straight lines between two points, because only one line can be straight and all others must be more or less curved to the extent that they depart from that straight line. Thus it is clear that this indifference of will has no place in God because it would be an imperfection. For this reason God is both a most free agent and a most necessary one, so that he must do whatever he does to and for his creatures since his infinite wisdom, goodness, and justice are a law to him which cannot be superseded.[h]

S. 3. Therefore it clearly follows that God was not indifferent about whether or not to give being to creatures, but he made them from an inner impulse of his divine goodness and wisdom. And so he created worlds and creatures as quickly as he could, for it is the nature of a necessary agent to do as much as he can. Since he could have created worlds or creatures from time immemorial, before the year six thousand or sixty thousand or six hundred thousand, it follows that he has done this. Therefore God can do anything which does not imply a contradiction. It is no contradiction if worlds or creatures are said to have been or to have existed continuously for an infinite time before this moment or after this moment. For, if there is no contradiction in the latter case, there is no contradiction in the former for the same reason.

S. 4. When these divine attributes have been duly considered, it also follows that an infinity of worlds or creatures was made by God. For since God is infinitely powerful, there can be no number of creatures to which he could not always add more. And, as has now been proven, he does as much as he can. Certainly his will, goodness, and kindness are as full and far-reaching as his power. Thus it clearly follows that his creatures are infinite and created in an infinity of ways, so that they cannot be bounded or limited by number or measure. Let us suppose, for example, that the whole universe of creatures is circular and that half its diameter contains as many diameters of the earth as there are grains of dust or sand in the entire world. If the universe were divided into such tiny atoms that one hundred thousand were contained in a single poppy seed, who could deny that the infinite power of God could make this number greater and greater by multiplying to infinity, since it is easier for this infinite power to multiply the real essences of creatures than for a skilled mathematician to make an even greater number, which can never be so great that it cannot be increased to infinity by addition or multiplication? Since it has already been demonstrated that God is a necessary agent and that he does

[h] See *Philosophicae Kabbalisticae Dissertatio*, ch. 6 & 7, *Kabbala Denudata*, i, pt. 3.

16

everything that he can do, it follows that he has multiplied and always multiplies and increases the essences of creatures to infinity.[i]

S. 5. The same argument shows that not only the entire universe or system of creatures as a whole is infinite or has infinity in itself, but even every creature, no matter how small, which we can see with our eyes or conceive of in our minds, has in itself such an infinity of parts or rather of entire creatures that they cannot be counted. Since it cannot be denied that God can place one creature inside another, he could therefore place two as easily as one, or four as easily as two, or eight as easily as four, so that he would thereby multiply them endlessly by always placing smaller creatures inside larger ones. And since no creature could be so small that a lesser one could not exist, so no creature is so big that a larger one could not always exist. It then follows that an infinite number of creatures can be contained and exist inside the smallest creatures and that all these could be bodies and in their own way mutually impenetrable. As for those creatures which are spirits and which can penetrate each other, there can be an infinite number of spirits in any created spirit, all of which spirits are as equal in extension to the aforementioned spirit as they are to each other. For in this case those spirits are more subtle and spiritual which penetrate grosser and more corporeal ones. Thus, there can be no lack of space so that one must give way to another. More will be said about the nature of bodies and spirits in the proper place. Here it is sufficient to demonstrate that in every creature, whether spirit or body, there is an infinity of creatures, each of which contains an infinity in itself, and so on to infinity.

S. 6. All these things especially praise and commend the great power and goodness of God because his infinity shines forth in the works of his hands, indeed, in every creature he has made. Nor can it be objected that we creatures stand as equals to God, for just as one infinity is greater than another, so God is always infinitely greater than all his creatures, so that nothing can be compared to him. And thus the truly invisible attributes of God are clearly seen if they are understood either through or in those things which have been made. The greater and more magnificent his works, the more they show the greatness of the maker. Therefore those who claim that the number of creatures in the universe is finite and only consists of so many individuals as can be numbered, and that the whole body of the universe occupies so many acres or miles or diameters of the earth in length, depth, and breadth, reckon the great majesty of God according to a paltry and unseemly scale. The God they imagine is not the true God but an idol of their own imagination, whom they confine to a narrow space, like the tiny cage of an imprisoned little bird, which is the width of a few fingers. For what else is that world which they imagine in comparison to that true and great universe described above?

[i] Concerning infinity, see *Philosophiae Kabbalisticae Dissertatio*, i, ch. 6, *Kabbala Denudata*, i.

S. 7. Furthermore, if they say that they do not confine God in this finite universe, but that they imagine him to exist no less outside this universe in infinite imaginary spaces and also within it, one may answer as follows. If these spaces are merely imaginary, they are nothing but the most idle conceits of the brain. But if they are real entities, what else can they be but creatures of God? Moreover, God works either in these spaces or not. If not, God is not there, for wherever he is, there he works since it is his nature to act, just as it is the nature of fire to burn or the sun to shine. For God always works, and his work is to create and to give being to creatures according to that eternal idea or wisdom that is in him. According to the Hebrews, the infinite God, whom they call *Aensoph*, is said to exist outside the place of the world because a creature could not comprehend the immensity of his light. (See what is said in the annotations to the first chapter.) Nor can he be said to exist in imaginary spaces, because evidently no space coincides with God, yet he can be said to act there through his own simple power. Whatever he does for creatures is done through the Messiah, who is not limitless like *Aensoph*.

S. 8. Moreover this continual action or operation of God, insofar as it is in him, proceeds from him, or insofar as it refers to himself, is only one continual action or command of his will; it has no succession or time in it, no before or after, but is always simultaneously present to God so that nothing is past or future because he has no parts. But insofar as it is manifested in or terminates in creatures, it is temporal and has a succession of parts. And although the imagination and understanding conceives this with difficulty, true and solid reason sufficiently affirms it. A common and humble example, such as follows, may offer some slight assistance to our understanding. Suppose a great circle or wheel to move about its center, which always remains still in that one place. In the same way, the sun is moved around its center by some angel or spirit who is in its center, within the space of so many days. Now, although the center moves the whole and produces a great and continual motion, it nevertheless remains always still and is not moved in any way. How much greater is this true of God, who is the first mover of all his creatures according to all their true and appointed motions. He, however, is not moved by them. Indeed, that which in God corresponds by analogy to the motions and operations of creatures is the rule of his own will. But if we wish to speak properly, there is no motion because all motion is successive and can have no place in God, as has been shown above.

S. 9. Against what we have said, namely that the smallest creatures which can be conceived have an infinite number of creatures within themselves so that the smallest particles of body or matter can be extended or divided in infinite ways into ever smaller and smaller parts, the following objection has been made by certain people. Whatever is actually divisible, if divided as far as any actual division can go, is divisible into indiscerpible parts.[2] Moreover, matter or body (matter, to be sure, is one thing or composed of many things) is actually divisible as far as actual division can go. Therefore, *et cetera*. I reply: This argument suffers from the fallacy which logicians call comparing incomparables, namely, joining words or terms which imply contradiction or absurdity, and this fallacy is hidden in this term "actually divisible," which denotes that one and the same thing is and is not divided. For "actually" signifies division and "divisible" signifies not division but the capacity for something to be divided, which is so absurd and contradictory that it is as if someone should say "visibly blind," "sensibly insensible," or "vivaciously dead." If, however, by the terms "actually divisible" they mean not two things but only one, namely either that which has truly been divided or that which is indeed divisible, the fallacy will be readily apparent to us. For, first, if the "actually divisible" denotes nothing to them except what has been divided in this sense, then I concede the major premise, namely that what is truly divided, insofar as there can be an actual division, is divisible into indiscerpible parts. But if this is so, the minor premise is false, namely that matter is actually divided to the extent that no further division can actually be made. Secondly, if by the term "actually divisible" they mean that a thing is only divisible or has the potential or capability to be divided, then I deny the major premise, namely that what is divisible, inasfar as it can be divided, is divisible into indiscerpible parts. And furthermore, in this sense the proposition is a mere tautology and an inane repetition of the same thing, such as the following: Whatever can be removed from its place, insofar as it can be removed, can be removed only up to a certain distance; but London or Rome can be removed from their own locations as far as they can be removed. Therefore, *et cetera*. It can be proven by the same form of argument that the soul of man has a finite number of years during which it exists or has its essence and that consequently it is mortal and has an end, as follows: That entity, whose time or duration is actually divisible to the extent to which an actual division can be made, will have an end and is divisible into a finite number of years; but the time or duration of the soul is actually divisible to the point where actual division cannot be continued any further. Therefore, *et cetera*. Should one object that if the duration of the soul reaches such a division of years it will

---

[2] i.e. "indivisible." "Indiscerpible" is a key word in Henry More's writings. He believed that matter was compounded of "indiscerpible" atoms of inert, passive matter, which had to be moved by spiritual forces. As he says: "I will define therefore a Spirit in generall thus, *A Substance penetrable and indiscerpible*. The fitness of which Definition will be the better understood, if we divide *Substance* in generall into these first kindes, viz. *Body and Spirit*, and then define *Body* to be *A Substance impenetrable and discerpible*. Whence the contrary kind to this is fitly defined, *A Substance penetrable and indiscerpible*" (*The Immortality of the Soul*, 1659, ed. A. Jacob [Dordrecht: Kluwer, 1987], liii, 1, pp. 29–31). Lady Conway rejects this definition of matter and spirit for the same reasons she rejects Descartes' theory of matter; both are dualistic. From this passage, with its implicit criticism of More, one can see that Lady Conway was no longer his "heroine pupil."

indeed have an end, then the soul could exist at another time after this first time and so on to infinity. I reply in a similar way that matter, if it comes to such a division, may have an end of that division and that it could then allow another division after the first, and so on to infinity.

I would like to note here that when I say that the smallest particle of body or so-called matter is always divisible into even smaller parts to infinity, so that there can be no actual division in matter which cannot always be further divided or has the capacity to be further divided and so on without end, I would not prescribe what the absolute power of God will do or could do, as some people argue so inanely and crassly. But I would only suggest what the power of God does and will do, insofar as he operates in and with creatures in producing and generating all things, just as in all resolutions or divisions of bodies neither nature nor creation has ever divided any body in such small parts nor ever could so divide it that any of these parts would not be capable of further division. Moreover, the body of any creature can never be reduced to its smallest parts. Indeed, it cannot be reduced either through the most subtle operations of any creature or created power. And this answer is sufficient for our purpose. For God does not make divisions in any body or matter except insofar as he works together with his creatures. Therefore he never reduces creatures into their smallest parts because all motion and operation would then cease in those creatures (for it is the nature of all motion that it breaks down and divides something into finer parts). To do this would be contrary to the wisdom and goodness of God. For if every motion or operation would cease in some creature, that creature would be entirely useless in creation and would be no better than if it were pure nothingness and utter non-being. Moreover, as has already been said, it is contrary to the wisdom and goodness of God or any of his attributes for him to be unable to do something. (The division of things is never in terms of the smallest mathematical term but of the smallest physical term. And when concrete matter is so divided that it disperses into physical monads, such as it was in the first state of its formation, then it is ready to resume its activity and become spirit just as happens with our food.)[j]

S. 10. Moreover, a consideration of the infinite divisibility of everything into always smaller parts is not an inane or useless theory, but of the very greatest use for understanding the causes and reasons of things and for understanding how all creatures from the highest to the lowest are inseparably united one to another by their subtler mediating parts, which come between them and which are emanations from one creature to another, through which they can act upon one another at the greatest distance. This is the basis of all the sympathy and antipathy which occurs in creatures, and if these things are well understood by someone, he may easily see into the most secret and hidden causes of most things, which ignorant men call occult qualities.

[j] Concerning the production of matter, see *Kabbala Denudata*, i, 2, pp. 310 ff. & ii, last tract, par. 28–9.

Chapter IV

S. 1. Whether God created all creatures at the same time or successively. S. 2. That all things are contained in Christ, the man, and have their essential being in him. S. 3. That Christ is, insofar as he is man, the first born of all creatures. S. 4. That no creature can ever attain equality with him.

S. 1. From what has been said above, this perplexing question can easily be answered, namely whether God created all creatures at the same time or one after the other? For, if the word "to create" refers to God himself or to an internal decree of his will, then creation occurred all at one time. But if "to create" refers to the creatures, then it occurred successively over time. For just as it is the nature and essential attribute of God to be immutable and eternal, so it is the nature of his creatures to be mutable and temporal. Finally, if the word "to create" refers to the universal seeds and principles, which are like springs and fountains from which creatures flow forth in an orderly succession determined by God (who is the greatest and first principle of all things), then it can also be said that all creatures were created at the same time, especially if one considers the Messiah or Christ, who is the first born of all creatures, through whom all things are said to have been made, as John declares, and as Paul expressly affirms, "through Christ all things visible and invisible have been made" (Colossians 1:16).

S. 2. Moreover, Jesus Christ signifies the whole Christ, who is God and man. As God, he is called *logos ousios*, or the essential word of the father. As man, he is the *logos proforikos*, or the word which is uttered and revealed, the perfect and substantial image of God's word, which is eternally in God and perpetually united to him so that it is his vehicle and organ, just like the body in respect to the soul. The New Testament and the Old Testament mention this revealed word, which is the wisdom of God, in different passages: Proverbs 8:22, 31 & 3:19; Psalms 33: 6 & 22: 2 & Psalm 110, pt. 1; Job 1: 1, 2, 3, etc.; Ephesians 3: 9. The passage in Colossians 1: 15–17 contains an explanation of the first truth, namely that through the Son or the word or wisdom neither God himself nor any of his attributes can be directly known. For how can the invisible image of God be designated by any of his attributes since they are as invisible as he is? For an image signifies something which has been made visible and which represents and reveals in some unique way the invisible God rather than any of his creatures.

S. 3. And for the same reason, Christ is called the first of all created beings by Paul in the passage cited above, where he describes the relation of Christ to creatures, who, in their primitive state, were all like the sons of God. At that time he was the first born of all the sons, and they were like the sons of that first-born son of God. This is why it is said that all things are contained in him and have their existence in him, because they arise from him just like branches from a root, so that they remain forever in him in a certain way.

S. 4. The creatures could not be equal to Christ nor of the same nature because his nature could never degenerate like theirs and change from good into bad. For this reason they have a far inferior nature in comparison to the first born, so that they can never strictly speaking become him, just as he can never become the Father. Moreover, the highest point they can reach is this, to be like him, as Scripture says. Consequently, inasmuch as we are only creatures, our relation to him is only one of adoption.

Chapter V

S. 1. That the ancient Kabbalists recognized the first-born son of God, whom they called the celestial Adam, the first Adam, the great priest. S. 2. That Christ is the mediator between God and all creatures. S. 3. That such a being is a mediator is as demonstrable from the principles of sound reason as is the existence of God. S. 4. That God is as immediately present in Christ as in all creatures. S. 5. That Christ cannot become evil but he can become good and consequently he partakes both of divinity and creatureliness as well as eternity and time. S. 6. That neither Christ nor those who are perfectly united with him are subject to the laws of time insofar as time signifies the destruction of things. S. 7. In this sense, we can be said to transcend time and rise above it into a higher region.

S. 1. Although some things have already been said in the previous chapter about the son of God, who is the first born of all creatures, nevertheless many things remain to be said about this matter which are necessary for the correct understanding of what follows; hence for that reason we write this chapter. By the son of God (the first born of all creatures, whom we Christians call Jesus Christ, according to Scripture, as shown above) is understood not only his divinity but his humanity in eternal union with the Divinity; that is, his celestial humanity was united with the Divinity before the creation of the world and before his incarnation. The ancient Kabbalists have written many things about this, namely, how the son of God was created; how his existence in the order of nature preceded all creatures; how everything is blessed and receives holiness in him and through him, whom they call in their writings the celestial Adam, or the first man Adam Kadmon, the great priest, the husband or betrothed of the church, or as Philo Judaeus[3] called him, the first-born son of God.

---

[3] Philo (c. 20 BC–c. 50 AD) was an Alexandrian Jewish philosopher. He took the Mosaic law as the foundation of philosophy but held that God had created the world indirectly through his potencies and attributes. All beings between the perfection of God and imperfect, finite matter have their

S. 2. This son of God, the first born of all creatures, namely this celestial Adam and great priest, as the most learned Jews call him, is, properly speaking, the mediator between God and the creatures. The existence of such a mediator is as demonstrable as the existence of God, as long as such a being is understood to be of a lesser nature than God and yet of a greater and more excellent nature than all remaining creatures. On account of his excellence he is rightly called the son of God.[k]

S. 3. As proof of this, namely, the existence of Christ as mediator, the following things must be considered: first, the nature or essence of God, the highest being; second, the nature and essence of the creatures, which are so unlike each other that the nature of this mediator will become immediately apparent to us. As has already been shown above, the nature and essence of God is altogether unchangeable, as sacred Scripture and our understanding, which has been placed in our minds by God, shows us. Therefore, if there were any mutability in God, it is necessary that it would tend towards the utmost measure and degree of goodness. In this case, however, he would not be the highest good, which is a contradiction. Furthermore, if anything proceeds to a greater degree of goodness, this is only because there is some greater being whose virtue and influence it shares. Now, there is no greater being than God, and he cannot improve or be made better in any way, much less decrease, which would imply his imperfection. Therefore it is clear that God, or the highest being, is wholly unchangeable. Moreover, since the nature of creatures is really distinct from the nature of God, inasmuch as he has certain attributes which cannot be communicated to his creatures, among which attributes is unchangeableness, it necessarily follows that creatures are changeable because otherwise they would be God himself. Indeed, daily experience teaches us that creatures are mutable and continually change from one state to another. Moreover, there are two kinds of change. One has the intrinsic power of changing itself either for good or bad, and this is common to all creatures, but not to the first born of all creatures. The other kind of change is the power of moving only from one good to another. Therefore there are three kinds of being. The first is altogether immutable. The second can only change toward the good, so that which is good by its very nature can become better. The third kind is that which, although it was good by its very nature, is nevertheless able to change from good to good as well as from good to evil. The first and last of these three kinds are opposites. The second is the natural medium between them, through which the extremes are united. It is therefore the most fitting and appropriate mediator, for it partakes of one

---

[k] Concerning this son of God, who is called *Adam Kadmon* by the Jews, many things are said in the *Kabbala Denudata*, i, pt. 1, pp. 28, 30; pt. 2, pp. 37 ff.; pt. 3, pp. 31–64; ii, pt. 3, pp. 244 & last tract, pp. 6, 7–26.
unity in, and proceed from, the divine Logos. These teachings had a profound influence on many Jewish and Christian writers, including Lady Conway.

extreme because it is mutable in respect to going from good to a greater degree of good and of the other extreme because it is entirely incapable of changing from good to bad. Such a mediator is necessary by the very nature of things because otherwise a gap would remain and one extreme would have been united with the other extreme without a mediator, which is impossible and against the nature of things, as is apparent throughout the entire universe. Here I am speaking about the moral, not the natural, immutability of the Messiah. Some people object that if Christ had been naturally immutable, then he was tempted in vain. (See Matthew 4: 3; Hebrews 2: 17, 18, 4: 15.) But there are other purely philosophical arguments that only the perfect first born emanated immediately from God at the beginning.[1] This is also confirmed in chapters II and VII by the authority of ancient and modern philosophers, along with a response to opposing arguments.

S. 4. This mediating being must not be understood in so crass a way, as if it stood at a midpoint between two extremes, just as the trunk of the body is between the head and the feet, but it is a median in respect to its nature, just as silver is a median between tin and gold, and water a median between air and earth. But these comparisons are quite gross in relation to the matter being discussed. For no one supposes that the son is the kind of intermediary between God and creatures, which implies that God himself is not immediately present in all creatures. Indeed, he is immediately present in all things and immediately fills all things. In fact, he works immediately in everything in his own way. But this must be understood in respect to that union and communication which creatures have with God so that although God works immediately in everything, yet he nevertheless uses this same mediator as an instrument through which he works together with creatures, since that instrument is by its own nature closer to them. Nevertheless, because that mediator is far more excellent in terms of its own nature than all the other created beings which we call creatures, it is rightly called the first born of all creatures and the son of God rather than a creature of God. And he comes into existence by generation or emanation from God rather than by creation strictly speaking, although according to a broader meaning and use of this word he can be said to have been created or formed, as the Scriptures say about him somewhere. But if the matter is correctly understood, then it is futile to argue about words. Nevertheless, the son of man is said to have been generated by God rather than made or created. We do not say that a house or ship is the son of its maker but, instead, is his work since the son is his living image and likeness, which cannot be said of a house or a ship. Thus, the first creation produced outside of God is more fittingly and properly called his son rather than his creature, because this is his living image and greater and more excellent than all creatures. It follows, moreover, that the son himself is

---

[1] Thirteen of these are presented in the *Kabbala Denudata*, i, pt. 3, Dissertatio 2, ch. 1.

immediately present in all these creatures so that he may bless and benefit them. And since he is the true mediator between God and his creatures, it follows, since he exists among them, that he raises them by his action to union with God. And since he is the most excellent creature produced outside of God as well as his most exact and perfect image, it is necessary that he is like God in all his attributes, which can be said without contradiction to have been communicated to Christ. Consequently, he must be present everywhere. Besides, if he were not present everywhere in all creatures, there would be an utter chasm and gap between God and creatures in which God would not exist. This is absurd.

S. 5. Besides, since he shares in the immutability of God and the mutability of the creatures, he is thus midway between that which is altogether immutable and that which is altogether mutable, participating in both. So he can be said to share eternity (which belongs to God) and time (which belongs to creatures), and although, as said above, nothing comes between eternity and time or between creatures and the will of God, which created these things, nevertheless "time" and "creature" must be understood in a broader sense, namely, in respect to all the things that God created outside of himself. Thus, this mediating being is included in God, just as in all other beings. For we cannot imagine that this mediating being existed in time before creatures, but only that he preceded them in the order of nature, so that, strictly speaking, there was no time between creatures and the all-creating power and will of God, which created them.

S. 6. However, if by "time" we mean, according to the ordinary sense of the word, a successive increase or decrease of things during which they grow for a certain period and then decline until they die or change into another state, in this sense one can say that neither this mediating being nor any creature perfectly united to God is subject to time and to its laws. For the laws of time extend only to a certain period or age, and when that period is completed, those things subject to time decline, waste away, and die or change into another kind of thing altogether according to the old saying: "Time, the devourer of things, and you, envious age, destroy everything."[4] For this reason time is divided into four parts, following the ages of men living in this world. These are infancy, youth, manhood, and old age. Thus, everything which ends in time and is subject to death and corruption or changes into something else, just as we see water change into stone, stones into earth, earth into trees, and trees into animals or living creatures.

But in that most excellent, mediating being there is neither defect nor corruption, and death, properly speaking, has no place in him. And he is like a most powerful and efficacious balm, through which all things are preserved from decline and death, and whatever is joined and united with him is always

---

[4] Ovid, *Metamorphosis*, Bk. XV. 234 ff.

new, lively, and growing. Here is perpetual youth without old age but with the virtues of age, namely, great increase of wisdom and experience without any of the imperfections of senility.

Yet when Christ became flesh and entered his body, which he brought with him from heaven (for every created spirit has some body, whether it is terrestrial, aerial, or etherial), he took on something of our nature and, consequently, of the nature of everything (because the nature of man contains the nature of all creatures, which is why he is called a microcosm). In assuming flesh and blood, he sanctified nature so that he could sanctify everything, just as it is the property of a ferment to ferment the whole mass. Then he descended into time and for a certain period willingly subjected himself to its laws to the extent that he suffered great torment and death itself. But death did not detain him long, for on the third day he rose again, and the purpose of all his suffering, up to his death and burial, was to heal, preserve, and restore creatures from corruption and death, which came upon them through the Fall, and so thereby put an end, at last, to time and raise creatures beyond time to himself, where he dwells, he who is the same yesterday, today, and forever, without loss, corruption, or death. Similarly, through his spiritual and inward appearance in men he saves, preserves, and restores their souls, and, as it were, subjects himself to suffering and death, and for a certain period he submits himself to the laws of time so that he may raise the souls of men above time and corruption up to himself, in whom they receive blessing and in whom they grow by degrees in goodness, virtue, and holiness forever.

S. 7. For this reason, those who achieve a perfect union with Christ are raised to a region of perfect tranquillity, where nothing is seen or felt to move or be moved. For although the strongest and swiftest motions exist there, nevertheless because they move so uniformly, equally, and harmoniously, without any resistance or disturbance, they appear completely at rest. Many examples of this can be found in the external world. For there are two kinds of rest which seem to our bodily sense of sight to lack motion, namely, that which is extremely swift and rapid and that which is very slow. Consequently we can only perceive the middle kind. Therefore, included in the laws of time are not only earth and earthly things but also the sun, moon, stars, and all the visible parts of the universe with many things which are invisible. Consequently, after some period of time all these things can change into very different kinds of things, and this happens through the same process and order of that divine operation which God gave to all things as law or justice. For in his divine wisdom he has decided to reward every creature according to its works. But enough has now been said about this most excellent mediating being, whom we will have occasion to mention in the following pages.

Chapter VI

S. 1. That all creatures are mutable in respect to their natures. S. 2. To what point this mutability extends, whether to the essential nature of things or only to their attributes and modes of being? S. 3. That only the modes of being are mutable but not the essences. S. 4. That there are only three kinds of being essentially distinct from each other, namely, God, who is supreme, Christ, the mediator, and creatures, who are lowest. S. 5. That these distinctions are very necessary and protect us from falling into either of the extreme positions which are available to us – one of which is Ranterism,[5] the other crass ignorance, both of which obscure the glory of the divine attributes. S. 6. An example of this is given. S. 7. That the justice of God gloriously appears in the transmutation of things from one species to another. S. 8. That when the human spirit changes itself through impiety into the qualities and conditions of animals, it is according to God's justice that the animal-like spirit enters the body of the animal and is punished there for some length of time. S. 9. How many erroneous ideas there are about God and how men conceive of God erroneously. S. 10. Why the world was first destroyed by water and must finally be destroyed by fire; and that all these punishments are medicinal. S. 11. That every creature is made of body and spirit, and in what way every creature, just as it has many bodies within itself, also has many spirits under one predominant general spirit, which rules all the others.

S. 1. Since all creatures are mutable in respect to their natures, the difference between God and creatures, rightly considered, is clearly demonstrated by daily experience. Now, if any creature is mutable in respect to its nature, it is mutable inasmuch as it is a creature. Consequently, all creatures are mutable according to the same law, namely, that whenever one thing is like another insofar as it belongs to one or another species, it is like everything contained in that species.

---

[5] The Ranters were seventeenth-century English political and religious radicals. They were pantheists and antinomians, meaning they rejected conventional standards of morality and believed those who were spiritually enlightened were above the law. They advocated total freedom of thought.

In fact, since mutability is appropriate for a creature insofar as it is a creature (this is the most general name of the species which includes all creatures), it appears that there is no other distinction between God and creatures. For if any creature were by its nature immutable, it would be God since immutability is one of his incommunicable attributes.

S. 2. Now let us consider the extent of this mutability. First, can one individual be changed into another, either of the same or of a different species? I say that this is impossible, for then the essential nature of things would change, which would cause great confusion not only for creatures but also for the wisdom of God, which made everything. For example, if one man could change into another, namely Paul into Judas or Judas into Paul, then he who sinned would not be punished for that sin but another in his stead who was innocent and virtuous. Thus a righteous man would not receive the reward of his virtue but another steeped in vice. But if we suppose that one righteous man is changed into another, as Paul into Peter and Peter into Paul, then Paul would surely not receive his proper reward but that of Peter, nor would Peter receive his but that of Paul. This confusion would not suit the wisdom of God. Besides, if the essential nature of individuals could change one into another, it would follow that creatures would not have a true being inasmuch as we could not be certain of anything nor could we have true knowledge or understanding of anything. Therefore all the innate ideas and precepts of truth, which all men find in themselves, would be false and, consequently, so would the conclusions drawn from them. For all true science or certainty of knowledge depends on the truth of objects, which we commonly call objective truths. If these objective truths were interchangeable, then the truth of any statement made about the object would also change. Therefore no statement could be invariably true, not even the clearest and most obvious, for example, the following: that the whole is greater than its parts and that two halves make a whole.

S. 3. Furthermore, we must consider whether one species can change into another. But first we must distinguish as carefully as possible how one species differs from another. For there are many species which are commonly said to differ, but nevertheless are not distinct from each other in substance or essence, but only in certain modes or attributes. And when these modes or attributes change, the thing itself is said to have changed its species. But indeed, it is not the essence or entity itself but only its mode of being which thus changes. For example, water does not change but stays the same, although when cold it freezes, where it was fluid before. When water turns to stone, there is no reason to suppose that a greater change of substance has occurred than in the earlier example when it changed from water to ice. And when a stone changes back into softer and more pliant earth, this too is no change of substance. Thus, in all other changes which can be observed the substance or essence always remains the same. There is merely a change of form inasmuch as the substance relinquishes one form and takes on another. These arguments prove that in terms of its substance or essence one species cannot change from one into another and equally that one individual cannot change into another. For species are nothing but individual entities subsumed under one general and common idea of the mind or one common term, as, for instance, man is a species including all individual men and horse is a species including all individual horses. If one man cannot change into another, much less can that man change into an individual of another species. Thus, if Alexander cannot change into Darius, he also cannot change into his own horse, Bucephalus.

S. 4. Since we know to what extent things are able to change, we must now determine how many species of things there are which are distinguished from each other in terms of their substance or essence. If we look closely into this, we will discover there are only three, which, as was said above, are God, Christ, and creatures; and that these three species are really distinct in terms of their essence has already been proved. No argument can prove that there is a fourth species distinct from the other three. Indeed, a fourth species seems altogether super-fluous. Since all phenomena in the entire universe can be reduced to these three aforementioned species as if into their original and peculiar causes, nothing compels us to recognize a further species according to this rule: whatever is correctly understood is most true and certain.[6] Entities should not be multiplied without need. Furthermore, because the three aforementioned species exhaust all the specific differences in substances which can possibly be conceived by our minds, then that vast infinity of possible things is fulfilled in these three species. How could a place or space be found for a fourth, fifth, sixth, or seventh species? It has already been shown that these three species have this capacity. Certainly insofar as something can be called an entity, it is either altogether immutable like God, the supreme being, or altogether mutable, that is for good or bad, like a creature, which is the lowest order of being, or partly mutable in respect to good, like Christ, the son of God, the mediator between God and creatures. In what category then could we place some fourth, fifth, sixth, or seventh, etc. species which is not clearly immutable or clearly mutable, nor partly mutable nor partly immutable. Besides, whoever posits some fourth species distinct from the previously mentioned three in terms of essence or substance destroys, in fact, the most excellent order which we find in the universe, since there would be not only one mediator between God and creatures but two, three, four, five, six, or however many can be imagined between the first and the last. Further-more, since it agrees with sound reason and with the order of things that just as God is one and does not have two or three or more distinct substances in himself, and just as Christ is one simple Christ without further distinct substances in himself (insofar as he is the celestial man or Adam, the first of all

---

[6] Here Lady Conway is adapting elements of Descartes' famous "method" for her own purposes.

creatures), so likewise all creatures, or the whole of creation, are also a single species in substance or essence, although it includes many individuals gathered into subordinate species and distinguished from each other modally but not substantially or essentially. Thus, what Paul says about human beings can also be understood about all creatures (which in their primitive and original state were a certain species of human being designated according to their virtues, as will be shown), namely, that God made all tribes and troops of creatures from one blood. Surely this is the explanation of the following two things: that God made all tribes of human beings from one blood so that they would love one another and would be bound by the same sympathy and would help one another. Thus God has implanted a certain universal sympathy and mutual love into his creatures so that they are all members of one body and all, so to speak, brothers, for whom there is one common Father, namely, God in Christ or the word incarnate. There is also one mother, that unique substance or entity from which all things have come forth, and of which they are the real parts and members. And although sin has weakened this love and sympathy in creatures to an astonishing degree, nevertheless it has not altogether destroyed it.

S. 5. Having acknowledged the three previously mentioned types of being, and these three alone, which are completely noninterchangeable among each other, we will proceed securely in the middle way of truth concerning the nature of substance, leaving the greatest errors and confusion to the right and left. First, there are those who maintain that all things are one substance, of which they are the real and proper parts. These confuse God and his creatures, as if these two notions were only one essential thing, so that sin and the devils would be nothing but parts or the slightest modification of this divine being. From this come dangerous consequences. Although I would not want this to be taken badly by all those who have fallen into this opinion by mistake, I should warn my readers where such principles lead so that they might consider them better and avoid their absurdity. Second, there are others who maintain that there are two kinds of substance, God, that supreme and utterly immutable being, and creatures, the lowest and altogether mutable beings. These, moreover, do not sufficiently consider that excellent order, described above, which appears in all things. Since they might perhaps have observed elsewhere that in addition to the two extremes there is also a certain mediator which partakes of both, and this is Jesus Christ, whom the wiser among the Jews recognize, no less than some among the so-called Gentiles, maintaining that there is such a mediator, which they call by different names such as Logos, Son of God, first-born Son of God, Mind, Wisdom, the Celestial Adam, etc. And, thus, they also call him the eternal mediator.

If these matters are correctly considered, they will contribute greatly to the propagation of the true faith and Christian religion among Jews and Turks and other infidel nations; if, namely, it is agreed that there are equally strong reasons by which we can prove that there is a mediator between God and human beings, indeed, between God and all creatures, as there are for proving that there is a God and a creation. Therefore, those who acknowledge such a mediator and believe in him can be said truly to believe in Jesus Christ, even though they do not yet know it and are not convinced that he has already come in the flesh. But if they first grant that there is a mediator, they will indubitably come to acknowledge also, even if they are unwilling, that Christ is that mediator.

There are others, moreover, who multiply specific entities into their own distinct essences and attributes almost to infinity. This altogether upsets that exceptional order of things and quite obscures the glory of the divine attributes so that it cannot shine with its due splendor in creatures. For if a creature were entirely limited by its own individuality and totally constrained and confined within the very narrow boundaries of its own species to the point that there was no mediator through which one creature could change into another, then no creature could attain further perfection and greater participation in divine goodness, nor could creatures act and react upon each other in different ways.

S. 6. We shall illustrate these things with one or two examples. Let us first imagine a horse, a creature endowed by its creator with different degrees of perfection, such as not only bodily strength but also certain notions, so to speak, of how to serve his master. In addition, a horse exhibits anger, fear, love, memory, and various other qualities which are in human beings and which we can also observe in dogs and many other animals. Therefore, since the divine power, goodness, and wisdom has created good creatures so that they may continually and infinitely move towards the good through their own mutability, the glory of their attributes shines more and more. And this is the nature of all creatures, namely that they be in continual motion or operation, which most certainly strives for their further good (just as for the reward and fruit of their own labor), unless they resist that good by a willful transgression and abuse of the impartial will created in them by God. Now, I ask, to what further perfection or degree of goodness of being or essence does or can a horse attain after he has performed good services for his master and has done what was and is appropriate for such a creature? Is a horse a mere machine or dead matter, or does it indeed have some kind of spirit which possesses thought, sense, love, and various other properties which are appropriate to its spirit? If it has such a spirit – something which must clearly be conceded – what happens to this spirit when the horse dies? If it is said that it returns to life and obtains the body of another horse, so that it becomes a horse as it was before but stronger and more beautiful and with a better spirit than before, excellent! If it dies a second, third, or fourth time, does it˙always remain a horse, even though it becomes continuously better and more excellent, and how often does its spirit return? Now, I ask, whether the species of horse possesses such infinite perfection that a horse can always become better and better to infinity, yet always remain a horse? To be sure, it is almost common knowledge that this visible earth will not always remain in its present state, which can be proven by the best arguments. Therefore it necessarily follows that the continual generation of animals in their crass bodies will also cease. For, if the earth assumes another form and produces no more vegetation, then horses and similar animals will cease to be as they were before. Since they would not have their proper nourishment, they could not remain the same species. Nevertheless, they will not be annihilated, as it is easy to conclude, for how can anything be annihilated since the goodness of God towards his creatures always remains the same and since the preservation or continuation of his creatures is a constant act of creation? It is generally agreed, as has been demonstrated above, that God is a perpetual creator acting with as much freedom as necessity. Yet, if one replies that the earth will change, as suggested above, then horses and other animals would change their configurations along with the earth, and the earth would produce nourishment for them according to their new configurations because of their changed condition. I then ask whether the creatures remain the same species during such a change, or whether there is not indeed some future difference between this and that state, such as, for example, that between a horse and a cow, which is commonly recognized as a different species. Furthermore, I ask whether some species of creatures so excel others to infinity that a certain individual of one species always increases in perfection and comes closer to some other species, yet is never able to reach that species? For example, a horse approaches the species of human being in many ways more than many other creatures. Is human nature therefore infinitely different from the nature of a horse or only finitely? If this distance is finite, the horse will surely change eventually into a human being – to be sure, in respect to its spirit, for in respect to its body, the matter is obvious. If this distance is infinite, then a certain actual infinite excellence will be attributed to a human being of the lowest and meanest understanding, an excellence such as only accords with God and Christ but to no creature. For the highest excellence of a creature is to be infinite only in potentiality, not in actuality. That is, it is always able to become more perfect and more excellent to infinity, although it never reaches this infinity. For however far a certain finite being may progress, it is nevertheless always finite, although there are no limits to its progress. For instance, if we could ever attain the least minute of eternity or a similar part of an infinite duration, this would not be infinite but finite.

In saying this, we do not contradict what was said in chapter III about the infinity of creatures, for that does not concern their infinite goodness and excellence but only their number and size, neither of which may be numbered or measured by any understanding of a created intellect. Nevertheless, individual creatures are only finitely good and finitely distant in terms of species. However, they are also potentially infinite, that is, they are always capable of greater perfection without end. Thus if someone places a stairs which is infinitely long and has an infinite number of steps, nevertheless the steps are not infinitely distant from each other, for otherwise there would be no possibility of ascent or descent. Moreover, the steps in this example signify species which cannot be infinitely distant from each other, or from those which are closest to them. In fact, daily experience teaches us that various species change into each other: earth changes into water, water into air, air into fire or ether and, vice versa, fire into air, air into water, etc., and these are nevertheless distinct species. Similarly, stones change into metals and one metal into another. However, let no one say that these are only bare bodies and have no spirit. We observe the same thing not only in plants but in animals. Just as wheat and barley can change into each other and in fact often do so, which is well known to farmers in many countries, especially in Hungary where, if barley is sown, wheat grows. In other more barren places, and especially in rocky places such as are found in Germany, if wheat is sown, barley grows instead, and in other places barley becomes plain grass.[7] Among animals, moreover, worms change into flies, and beasts and fish that feed on beasts and fish of another species change into their nature and species. And does not rotting matter, or body of earth and water, produce animals without any previous seed of those animals?[8] And in the creation of this world did not the waters produce fish and birds at God's command? Did the earth not also at the same command bring forth reptiles and beasts, which were, on this account, real parts of earth and water? And just as they have their bodies from the earth, so they have their spirits, or souls, from the earth. For the earth produced living souls, as the Hebrew text says, and not simply material bodies lacking life and spirit. For this reason the difference between human beings and beasts is exceedingly striking. For it is said about human beings that God made them in his image and breathed into them the breath of life and they became living souls, so that they received his life, the principal part that makes them human beings, which is really distinct from the divine soul or spirit which God breathed into them.

Moreover, since the human body was made from earth, which, as has been proved, contained various spirits and gave those spirits to all the animals, without doubt the earth gave human beings the best and most excellent spirits which it contained. But all these spirits were far inferior to the spirit of human beings, which they received from above and not from the earth. The human spirit ought to have dominion over these spirits, which are only terrestrial, so that it might rule over them and raise them to a higher level and, indeed, to its

---

[7] Lady Conway never traveled in Germany or Hungary. These examples come from van Helmont's writings.

[8] Lady Conway accepts the traditional idea that animals were spontaneously generated from decaying matter. This idea was disproven by the microscopic observations of Marcello Malpighi (1628–94), among others.

own proper nature; and this would have been its true increase and multiplication. For their sake, it allowed the earthly spirits existing in it to have dominion over it, so that it would be like them. For this reason it is said, "You are of the earth and you shall return to earth," which has a spiritual as well as a literal meaning.

S. 7. We already see how the justice of God shines so gloriously in this transmutation of one species into another. For it is most certain that a kind of justice operates not only in human beings and angels but also in all creatures. Whoever does not see this must be called completely blind. This justice appears as much in the ascent of creatures as in their descent, that is, when they change for better or worse. When they become better, this justice bestows a reward and prize for their good deeds. When they become worse, the same justice punishes them with fitting penalties according to the nature and degree of their transgression. The same justice imposes a law for all creatures and inscribes it in their very natures. Whatever creature breaks this law is punished accordingly. But any creature who observes this law receives the reward of becoming better.

Thus under the law which God gave to the Jews, if a beast has killed a man, the beast had to be killed. A human life, it is said, is to be sought at the hand of every beast (Genesis 9: 5). If anyone has sexual dealings with a beast, not only the man but the beast must be killed. Thus, not only the wife and her husband (Adam and Eve) received a sentence and punishment from God after their transgression but also the serpent, which was the brute part in man that he took from the earth. God endowed man with the same instinct for justice towards beasts and the trees of the field. For any man who is just and good loves the brute creatures which serve him, and he takes care of them so that they have food and rest and the other things they need. He does not do this only for his own good but out of a principle of true justice; and if he is so cruel toward them that he requires work from them and nevertheless does not provide the necessary food, then he has surely broken the law which God inscribed in his heart. And if he kills any of his beasts only to satisfy his own pleasure, then he acts unjustly, and the same measure will be measured out to him. Thus, a man who has a tree in his orchard that is fruitful and grows well fertilizes and prunes it so that it becomes better and better. But if it is barren and a burden to the earth, he fells it with an ax and burns it. Therefore, there is a certain justice in all these things, so that in the very transmutation from one species to another, either by ascending from a lower to a higher or by descending in the opposite way, the same justice appears. For example, is it not just that if a man lives a pure and holy life on this earth, like the heavenly angels, that he is elevated to the rank of angels after he dies and becomes like them, since the angels also rejoice over him? However, a man who lives such an impious and perverse life that he is more like the devil raised from hell than like any other creature, then, if he dies in such a state without repenting, does not the same justice hurl him down to hell, and does he not justly become like the devils, just as those who live an angelic life become equal to angels? But if someone lives neither an angelic nor a diabolical life but rather a brutish or animal life, so that his spirit is more like the spirit of beasts than any other creature, does the same justice not act most justly, so that just as he became a brute in spirit and allowed his brutal part and spirit to have dominion over his more excellent part, he also (at least as regards his external shape) changes his corporeal shape into that species of beast to which he is most similar in terms of the qualities and conditions of his mind? And since that brute spirit is now superior and predominant and holds the other spirit captive, is it not likely that when such a man dies, his brute spirit always has dominion over him and takes away his human spirit and compels it to serve the animal spirit in every possible way? And when that brute spirit returns again into some other body, it rules over that body and has the ability and freedom to shape the body according to its own ideas and inclinations (which it did not previously have in the human body). It necessarily follows that this body, which the vital spirit forms, will be that of a brute and not a human, for the brute spirit cannot produce or form any other shape because its formative power is governed by its imagination, which imagines and conceives as strongly as possible its own image, according to which the external body must take shape.

S. 8. In this way the justice of God shines forth wonderfully, since it assigns the due and appropriate punishment for each kind and degree of wrongdoing nor does it demand hellfire and damnation for every single wicked sin and transgression. For Christ taught the opposite in that parable where he shows that only the third degree of punishment is to be sent down to Gehenna, as when one rashly says to his brother, "You fool!" (Matthew 5: 22).

What objection can be made to the justice of God? If it is said that the dignity and nobility of human nature is diminished and sullied when it is decreed that the body and soul is to be turned into the nature of a brute, one may reply according to the common axiom, "the worst corruption is that of the best." For when a human being has so greatly degraded himself by his own willful wrongdoing and has brought his nature, which had been so noble, to a lower state, and when that nature has demeaned itself in spirit to the level of a most foul brute or animal so that it is wholly ruled by lust and earthly desires and becomes like any beast, indeed, worse than any beast, what injustice is this if God compels him to bear the same image in his body as in that spirit into which he has internally transformed himself? Or which degeneration do you think is worse, to have the image of a beast in one's spirit or body? Certainly it must be said that to be like a brute in spirit is the greatest possible degeneration. There is hardly anyone with any genuine nobility of soul who does not admit that to be a brute internally is worse than to be a brute externally. For it is far worse to be a brute in spirit than to be a brute in outward form and shape. However, if someone says that it is too mild a punishment for those who have lived a brutal life throughout all their days merely to return after death in the condition and state of a beast, let them know that the most just creator and maker of all things is wiser than they and knows better what punishment is appropriate for each sin. God has arranged all things as justly and wisely as possible so that no one living carnally like a beast can enter the kingdom of heaven. Furthermore, Christ expressly teaches us that not every sin must be punished with the penalty of hell and that "where the treasure is, there also is the heart and spirit of man" (Matthew 6: 21). Also, if a man is united and joined with something, he then becomes one with that thing. He who unites himself to God is one with him in spirit, and he who unites himself to a prostitute is one in flesh with her. Shouldn't someone who is united to a beast become one with that beast for the same reason and similarly in every other case? For, according to Scripture, anyone who obeys another is his servant inasmuch as he obeys him. Besides, it is said that, "by whatsoever measure you shall measure, you shall be measured by the same" (Luke 6: 38). That is to say, that all degrees and kinds of sin have their appropriate punishments, and all these punishments tend toward the good of creatures, so that the grace of God will prevail over judgment and judgment turn into victory for the salvation and restoration of creatures. Since the grace of God stretches over all his work, why do we think that God is more severe and more rigorous a punisher of his creatures than he truly is? This obscures and darkens the glory of God's attributes in an astonishing way and does not foster love for God and admiration for his goodness and justice in the hearts of men as it should, but does precisely the opposite.

S. 9. For the common notion of God's justice, namely, that whatever the sin, it is punished by hellfire and without end, has generated a horrible idea of God in men, as if he were a cruel tyrant rather than an benign father towards all his creatures. If, however, an image of a lovable God was more widely known, such as he truly is and shows himself in all his dealings with his creatures, and if our souls could inwardly feel and taste him, as he is charity and kindness itself and as he reveals his intrinsic self through the light and spirit of our Lord Jesus Christ in the hearts of men, then, and only then, will men finally love God above everything and acknowledge him as the most loving, just, merciful God, fit to be worshipped before everything, and as one who cannot inflict the same punishment on all sinners.

S. 10. Then, why did he destroy the original world with water and decide to destroy this world with fire, such as happened with Sodom? Surely, to show that he uses different kinds of punishments for different kinds of sins. The first world was bad, and this one, which had to be destroyed by fire, would have been worse. For this reason it was to have a greater punishment. But the different nature of this transgression, for which different punishments have been devised, seems to consist in this, that the sins of the old world were more carnal and brutal, as the word of God reveals when he said, "My spirit will not always strive in man because he was made flesh" (Genesis 6: 3); that is, he was made completely brutal or bestial by obeying the desires of the flesh. Consequently, if that generation had not been wiped out, the whole human race (with the exception of Noah and his family) would have been bestial in the following generations, which evil God wished to avert by drowning them in water so that by this punishment they might revert from the nature of beasts to that of men. But the sins of this world, like those of Sodom, which had to be destroyed by fire, appear to be more like the sins of the devil than anything else because of their hostility, malice, cruelty, fraud, and cunning. Therefore their appropriate punishment is fire, which is the original essence of those so noble, yet degenerate, spirits, and by this same fire they must be degraded and restored.

For what is fire, but a certain kind of ethereal and imperfect substance enclosed in combustible bodies, which we always see ascend and immediately vanish because of its remarkable tenuousness? In regard to their spirits, angels as well as men originate from this ethereal substance, just as brutes originate from water. Just as all the punishments inflicted by God on his creatures are in proportion to their sins, so they tend, even the worst, to their good and to their restoration and they are so medicinal as to cure these sickly creatures and restore them to a better condition than they previously enjoyed.

S. 11. Now, let us consider briefly how creatures are composed and how the parts of this composition can change into one another because they originally had one and the same essence and being. In every visible creature there is body and spirit, or a more active and a more passive principle, which are appropriately called male and female because they are analogous to husband and wife. For just as the normal generation of human beings commonly requires the conjunction and cooperation of male and female, so too does every generation and production, whatever it may be, require the union and simultaneous operation of those two principles, namely spirit and body. Moreover, spirit is light or the eye looking at its own proper image, and the body is the darkness which receives this image. And when the spirit beholds it, it is as if someone sees himself in a mirror. But he cannot see himself reflected in the same way in clear air or in any diaphanous body, since the reflection of an image requires a certain opacity, which we call body. Nevertheless, it is not an essential property of anything to be a body, just as it is not a property of anything to be dark. For nothing is so dark that it cannot become bright. Indeed, darkness itself can become light. In the same way, light which is created can turn to darkness, as the words of Christ plainly show when he says, "If the light within you is darkness," etc., by which he means the eye or spirit which is in the body and which sees the image of something. Just as every spirit needs a body to receive and reflect its image, it also needs a body to retain the image. For every body has this retentive nature in itself to a greater or a lesser degree, and the more perfect a body is – that is, the more perfectly mixed it is – the more retentive it is. Thus water is more retentive than air, and earth is more retentive of certain things than water. The semen of a female creature, on account of its so perfect mixture, because it is the purest extract of the whole body, has a remarkable power of retention. In this semen, as in the body, the masculine semen, which is the spirit and image of the male, is received and retained together with the other spirits which are in the woman. And whatever spirit is strongest and has the strongest image or idea in the woman, whether male or female, or any other spirit received from outside of one or the other of them, that spirit predominates in the semen and forms a body as similar as possible to its image.[9] And thus every creature receives its external shape.

In the same way, the internal productions of the mind (namely the thoughts which are true creatures according to their kind and which have a true substance appropriate to themselves) are generated. These are our inner children, and all are masculine and feminine; that is, they have a body and spirit. For, if they did not have a body, they could not be retained nor could we reflect on our own thoughts. For all reflection takes place because of a certain darkness, and this is the body. Thus memory requires a body in order to retain the spirit of the thing conceived of; otherwise it vanishes, just as an image in a mirror immediately vanishes when the object is removed. Thus when we remember something, we see within ourselves its image, which is the spirit that proceeded from it, while we looked at it from the outside. This image, or spirit, is retained in some body, which is the semen of our brain. Thus a certain spiritual generation occurs in us. Consequently, every spirit has its own body and every body its own spirit. Just as a body, whether of a man or brute, is nothing but a countless multitude of bodies collected into one and arranged in a certain order, so the spirit of man or brute is also a countless multitude of spirits united in this body, and they have their order and government, such that one is the principal ruler, another has second place, and a third commands others below itself, and so on for the whole, just as in an army. For this reason, creatures are called armies and God the leader of these armies. Just as the devil, who assaulted the man, was called Legion because there were many of them. Thus every human being, indeed, every creature whatsoever, contains many spirits and bodies. (The many spirits which exist in men are called by the Jews Nizzuzuth, or sparks.)[m] Truly, every

---

[m] See *Kabbala Denudata*, ii, pt. 2, *De Revolutione Animarum*, pp. 255–68, etc.

[9] Lady Conway accepted the Galenic theory of reproduction. Galen was a second-century Roman physician, who believed that both males and females produced semen. During the seventeenth century this egalitarian view of reproduction was replaced by a revival of the Aristotelian view that only males produced semen. Therefore, while males contributed spiritual and mental characteristics to the fetus, the female contribution was limited to the physical and material. Analogies were drawn between the womb and an oven, in which bread was baked, or a field, in which seed was sown.

body is a spirit and nothing else, and it differs from a spirit only insofar as it is darker. Therefore the crasser it becomes, the more it is removed from the condition of spirit. Consequently, the distinction between spirit and body is only modal and incremental, not essential and substantial.

Chapter VII

S. 1. Every body can change into a spirit and every spirit into a body because the distinction between body and spirit is only one of mode, not essence. One reason for this comes from the order of things mentioned above, which consists in only three things. Even the worst creatures, the most dreadful demons, become good after many and long torments and punishments. Furthermore, this crassness and hardness of bodies arose after a fall, and on this account they will return to a subtle and supple state. S. 2. Another reason for this comes from the divine attributes, some of which can be communicated to all his creatures. S. 3. A third reason comes from the love which spirits have for bodies. S. 4. To be penetrable and indivisible applies as much to bodies as to spirits, and to be impenetrable and divisible is equally applicable to spirits as to bodies. For this reason, the difference is only one of degree not of essence, and no creature or created spirit can be intimately present in any other creature because intimate presence pertains to God and Christ alone. Therefore, that philosophical penetration of bodies by created spirits is a pure fiction of the Scholastics.

In order to demonstrate this a bit more clearly, namely, that every body is a certain life or spirit in nature and has the principle of perception, having sense and thought, love, desire, joy, and grief insofar as it is affected in one way or another, and consequently, that every body has activity and motion in itself so that it can move itself wherever it wants to be, I claim that every body in its own nature, as it was originally created and will be once again, will return to its primordial state and be freed from that confusion and vanity to which it is subjected on account of sin.[n]

S. 1. The first reason is derived from the aforementioned order of things which I have already shown to be only three, namely, God as the highest, Christ as the mediator, and the creation as the lowest rank of all. This creation is one entity or substance in respect to its nature or essence, as demonstrated above, so that it only varies according to its modes of existence, one of which is

---

[n] Concerning the nature of matter and spirit, more can be seen in *Kabbala Denudata*, i, pt. 2, pp. 308–12; ii, last tract, pp. 6, 28–9, 32.

corporeality. There are many degrees of this so that any thing can approach or recede more or less from the condition of a body or spirit. Moreover, because spirit is the more excellent of the two in the true and natural order of things, the more spiritual a certain creature becomes (that is, if it does not degenerate in other ways), the closer it comes to God, who, as we all know, is the highest spirit. Thus, a body is always able to become more and more spiritual to infinity since God, who is the first and highest spirit, is infinite and does not and cannot partake of the least corporeality. Consequently, it is the nature of a creature, unless it degenerates, always to become more and more like the creator. But because there is no being which is in every way contrary to God (surely nothing exists which is infinitely and immutably bad, as God is infinitely and immutably good, and there is nothing which is infinitely dark as God is infinitely light, nor is anything infinitely a body having no spirit, as God is infinitely spirit having no body), it is therefore clear that no creature can become more and more a body to infinity, although it can become more and more a spirit to infinity. And nothing can become darker and darker to infinity, although it can become brighter and brighter to infinity. For this reason, nothing can be bad to infinity, although it can become better and better to infinity. Thus, in the very nature of things there are limits to evil, but none to goodness. In the same way, every degree of evil or sin has its own punishment, pain, and chastisement appropriate to the nature of the deed itself, by means of which evil turns back again to good. Although the creature does not immediately recognize it when it sins, the punishment or chastisement adheres in the sins which creatures commit in such a way that it appears at the appropriate time. At this time every sin will have its own punishment and every creature will feel pain and chastisement, which will return that creature to the pristine state of goodness in which it was created and from which it can never fall again because, through its great punishment, it has acquired a greater perfection and strength. Consequently, from that indifference of will which it once had for good or evil, it rises until it only wishes to be good and is incapable of wishing any evil.°

Hence one can infer that all God's creatures, which have previously fallen and degenerated from their original goodness, must be changed and restored after a certain time to a condition which is not simply as good as that in which they were created, but better. The work of God cannot cease, and thus it is the nature of every creature to be always in motion and always changing from good to better and from good to evil or from evil back to good. And because it is not possible to proceed towards evil to infinity since there is no example of infinite evil, every creature must necessarily turn again towards good or fall into eternal silence, which is contrary to nature. But if anyone should say that it falls into eternal torment, I answer: if you understand by eternity an infinity of ages

° See *Kabbala Denudata*, ii, last tract, p. 61; sec. 9, p. 69, sec. 2 & 70, sec. 5 & tract 2, p. 157.

which will never end, this is impossible because all pain and torment stimulates the life or spirit existing in everything which suffers. As we see from constant experience and as reason teaches us, this must necessarily happen because through pain and suffering whatever grossness or crassness is contracted by the spirit or body is diminished; and so the spirit imprisoned in such grossness or crassness is set free and becomes more spiritual and, consequently, more active and effective through pain.

Thus, since a creature cannot proceed infinitely toward evil nor fall into inactivity or silence or utter eternal suffering, it irrefutably follows that it must return toward the good, and the greater its suffering, the sooner its return and restoration. And so we see how a certain thing, while always remaining the same substance, can change marvelously in respect to its mode of being, so that a holy and blessed spirit or an angel of light may become an evil and cursed spirit of darkness through its own willful actions. This change or metamorphosis is as great as if spirit changed into body. And if one asks whether these spirits become more corporeal than they previously were in their original state before they fell through their own wrongdoing, I answer, yes, since, as I have already shown, spirit is able to become more or less corporeal in many degrees, although not to infinity. By the same token, spirits can remain for long periods of time without any of the crassness of body characteristic of visible things in this world, such as hard stones or metals or the bodies of men and women. For surely the bodies of the worst spirits do not have the same crassness as a visible body. And yet all that crassness of visible bodies comes from the fall of the spirits from their original state. Because of this grossness, spirits can become contracted after long and varied periods of time, although they cannot together and at one time fall into a general grossness, such that the entire body of a fallen spirit can be equally crass in all its parts. But some parts become grosser and grosser, and the remaining parts of this corporeal spirit (these are the means by which spirit is intimately united to body) retain a certain tenuousness, without which spirit cannot be so active or mobile as otherwise. The principal spirit (together with its ministering spirits – as many as it can gather together – along with those subtle and tenuous parts of the body) departs from these crasser parts of the body, which it abandons as if they were so many dead corpses which are no longer fit to serve those same spirits in operations which they perform in their present state.

We see this excess of subtler and stronger spirits in an alcoholic liquor change from grosser and harder parts into better and more tenuous ones. Such a liquor freezes when the stronger spirits (having left behind the harder parts which are especially exposed to the outside cold) withdraw to the middle of the body which remains tenuous, so that every single drop of that liquor (which does not freeze but always remains liquid in the innermost parts of that frozen body) has in itself the multiplied strength of all those parts which are frozen. We must recognize that the grossness and hardness of bodies is twofold: one sort is visible and palpable to our external sense; the other is invisible and impalpable, but nevertheless just as gross as the other, indeed, often grosser and harder, since it can be perceived internally by our inner senses, although it does not affect our external senses. Therefore, invisible and impalpable grossness and hardness is characteristic of those bodies which are so slight that our external senses cannot perceive them. Nevertheless, they are extremely hard, harder in fact than any flint or metal which our hands can hold. For the most part, visible water is composed of these small, hard bodies, although it appears to us quite soft, fluid, and tenuous on account of the many other subtle bodies which continually stir and move the hard particles, so that to our crass senses water appears one simple, uniform, homogeneous thing. Nevertheless, it consists of many hetero- geneous and dissimilar parts, more so than most other bodies. Many of these parts are quite hard and rocky, from which come bubbling sands and all other sorts of gravel and stones, whose origin and birth arise from the water in the depths of the earth. When these little stones or those pebbly particles of water grow into visible gravel and stones, they lose this hardness after a certain period of time and become softer and more tenuous than when they were part of the water. For stones decay and turn into soft earth from which animals come forth. Thus, even decaying stones often turn back into water; but this is a different sort of water than before, for the first is becoming hard and the second becoming soft. By way of example, it has been observed that two kinds of water flow from one and the same mountain in Switzerland. Drinking one sort produces kidney stones, but the other provides a remedy against this. Thus, one kind of water turns to stone and the other comes out of stones when it putrefies and consequently loses its previous hardness and changes. From these examples one may easily understand how the heart or spirit of a wicked man is called hard and stony because his spirit has indeed real hardness in it like that found in those small, stony particles of water. On the other hand, the spirit of a good person is soft and tender. We can really sense the internal hardness and softness of spirit, and any good person perceives this as tangibly as he can feel the external hardness of crass, external bodies with his external touch. Moreover, those who are dead in their sins lack this sense of the hardness or softness of good or bad spirits, and for this reason they regard these phrases as merely metaphors, when, in fact, they have a real and proper meaning without any figurative sense.

S. 2. From a serious and due consideration of the divine attributes (from which the truth of everything can be made clear, as if from a treasure house stored with riches), I have deduced another reason why created spirits can change into bodies and bodies into spirits. For since God is infinitely good and communicates his goodness to all his creatures in infinite ways, so that there is no creature which does not receive something of his goodness, and this as fully as possible, and since the goodness of God is a living goodness, which possesses life, knowledge, love, and power, which he communicates to his creatures, how can any dead thing proceed from him or be created by him, such as mere body or matter, according to the hypothesis of those who affirm that matter cannot be changed into any degree of life or perception? It has been truly said that God does not make death. It is equally true that he did not make any dead thing, for how can a dead thing come from him who is infinite life and love? Or, how can any creature receive so vile and diminished an essence from him (who is so infinitely generous and good) that it does not share any life or perception and is not able to aspire to the least degree of these for all eternity? Did not God create all his creatures to this end, namely, that they be blessed in him and enjoy his divine goodness in their various conditions and states? Moreover, how could this be possible without life or perception? How can anything lacking life enjoy divine goodness? We will carry this argument even farther.

The divine attributes are commonly and correctly divided into those which are communicable and those which are not. The incommunicable are that God is a being subsisting by himself, independent, immutable, absolutely infinite, and most perfect. The communicable attributes are that God is spirit, light, life, that he is good, holy, just, wise, etc. Among these communicable attributes there are none which are not alive and life itself. And since every creature shares certain attributes with God, I ask what attribute produces dead matter, or body, which is incapable of life and sense for eternity? If one says that this conforms with God in his reality or in the fact that he has an essence, I reply: There can be no dead reality of which he is or could be a part, which would imply that he would have his own dead reality. Besides, reality is not properly speaking attributed to something; but what is properly attributed to something is what is predicated or affirmed about that reality. For what attributes or perfections can be assigned to dead matter which are analogous to those in God? If we inquire closely into this matter, we shall discover nothing at all, for every one of his attributes is alive, indeed, is life itself.

Moreover, since God's creatures, insofar as they are creatures, must be like their creator in certain things, I ask, in what way is this dead matter like God? If they say again, "to his pure reality," I reply: There can be nothing like that either in God or in creatures, and therefore it is simply non-being.

As for the remaining attributes of matter, namely, hardness, shape, and motion, these can obviously have no place in God. Consequently, they are not among his communicable attributes, but are rather the essential differences or various attributes by which creatures, as such, are distinguished from God, because mutability is also one of those differentiating attributes. Therefore one cannot say that mutability is one of God's communicable attributes. In the same way, hardness, shape, and motion are not among God's communicable attributes but only among those by which creatures differ from him. Since dead matter does not share any of the communicable attributes of God, one must then conclude that dead matter is completely non-being, a vain fiction and Chimera, and an impossible thing. If one should say that dead matter has metaphysical truth and goodness, to the extent that every being is true and good, again, I ask, what is this truth or goodness? For, if it shares nothing of the communicable attributes of God, it will not be true or good and, consequently, will be an utter fiction, as previously said. Furthermore, since one cannot say how dead matter shares in divine goodness in the least, one has even less chance of showing how it is capable of reason and able to acquire greater goodness to infinity, which is the nature of all creatures since they grow and progress infinitely toward greater perfection, as shown above. For what further progress in goodness and perfection can dead matter make? For after it has undergone infinite changes of motion and figure, it is forced to remain dead as before. And if motion and shape contribute nothing to life, then that matter can never improve or ever progress in goodness in the smallest degree. For suppose that this dead matter, or body, has assumed all forms and has been changed into all kinds of shapes, both the most regular and precise. What use is this body or matter since it lacks all life and perception? Thus we maintain that matter has assumed an infinity of motions from the slowest to the fastest, on account of which it becomes better by virtue of a certain inner power to improve itself. An argument for this intrinsic power is that the improvement is such as the nature of the thing requires and which it brings about. However, merely dead body and matter requires no kind of motion or shape, nor does it do anything for itself through one motion or shape more than another. For it is equally indifferent to every motion or shape whatsoever and, consequently, cannot be improved or perfected by any of them. And what benefit will come to it from all these helps, if it remains dead and passive?

S. 3. My third argument is drawn from that great love and desire which spirits or souls have for bodies, and especially for those bodies with which they are united and in which they dwell. Now, the basis of all love or desire, which brings one thing to another, is that they are of one nature and substance, or that they are like each other or of one mind, or that one has its being from another. We find examples of this among all animals which produce their own offspring in the same way as human beings. For they clearly love whatever they bring to birth. Thus even wicked men and women (if they are not extremely perverse and profligate) love their own children and cherish them with natural affection. The reason for this is surely that their children are of one nature and substance, as if they were part of them. And if their children look like them, either in body, spirit, or manner, love for them grows greater because of this. We also see that animals of the same species love each other more than animals of a different species. Thus cattle of one species graze together, birds of one species fly in flocks, fish of one species swim together, and men prefer to associate with men rather than with other creatures. In addition to this particular love, there is also a certain universal love in all creatures for each other, in spite of that great confusion which resulted from the Fall. This surely should follow from the same basic principle, that all things are one in virtue of their primary substance or essence and are like parts or members of the same body. Furthermore, we see in every species of animal that males and females love each other and that in all their matings (which are not monstrous and against nature) they care for each other. This comes not only from the unity of their nature but also because of their remarkable similarity to each other. There are two foundations for the love between men and women expressly mentioned in Genesis. One refers to the unity of their nature, for example, when Adam says of his wife: "She is bone of my bone, flesh of my flesh, etc." (Genesis 2: 23). For she was taken from him and was part of him and therefore loved him. The second refers to their similarity, because no helpmeet was found for him before she was made. As it says in Hebrew, among all creatures he saw no one like himself with whom he could associate, until Eve was created for him. But there is yet another reason for love, when beings which love each other are not one substance, but one has given being to another and is the genuine and real cause of it. So it is between God and the creatures. For he gave existence, life, and motion to everything and he therefore loves everything and is unable not to love everything. Indeed, when he appears to hate them and to be angry with them, this anger and what comes from it, namely, punishment and judgment, are for their good because he saw they needed them. Those creatures, on the other hand, which are not altogether degenerate and lost to every sense of God, love him. This is a certain divine law and instinct with which he has endowed all rational creatures so that they love him, which is the fulfillment of all the commandments. Moreover, those creatures which are most like God love him more and are more loved by him. But if one maintains that there is yet another reason for love, which is the principal one, namely, goodness, which is the strongest attraction of love and the reason why God must be loved as much as possible by all things because he is the best, then where there is also such goodness, either real or apparent, in his creatures, their fellow creatures love them. I answer that one must concede that goodness is the great, indeed, the greatest cause of love and its proper object. This goodness is not, however, a reason distinct from those already mentioned but included in them. For the reason why we call something good is because it really or apparently pleases us on account of its similarity to us, or ours to it. This is why good people love good people and not others. For good people cannot love bad people, nor bad people good. For there is no greater similarity than between good and good. Therefore, the reason why we call, or think, something good is that it does us good and we share its goodness. Consequently, similarity remains the first cause of love. Thus when anything gives being to another, as when God and Christ give being to creatures (indeed, true essence comes from them alone), they are similar to some extent. For it is impossible for a creature not to have some similarity to its creator or to agree with it in certain attributes and perfections.

Taking this as a touchstone, let us now return to our subject, that is, let us examine whether or not spirit and body are of one nature and substance and therefore able to change into each other? I ask, then, for what reason does the soul or human spirit so love the body and so unite with it and so unwillingly depart from it that, as is widely known, the souls of certain people remain with their bodies and in their power after the death of the body and until it decomposes and turns to dust. The reason for this love cannot be that the spirit or soul gave a distinct being to the body, or the body to the spirit, for this would be creation in a strict sense, properly speaking. Moreover, it is solely the function of God and Christ alone to give being to things. Therefore, love necessarily occurs because of the similarity or affinity between their natures. But if one says that there is a certain goodness in the body which moves the spirit to love it, then this goodness will necessarily correspond to something which is similar to it in the nature of the soul. Otherwise, the body could not be brought to the soul. Indeed, let them tell us, then, what is that goodness in the body on account of which the soul loves it so much? In what attributes or perfections is body similar to spirit, if the body is nothing but a dead trunk and a certain mass, which is altogether incapable of any life or degree of perfection? If they say that the body agrees with the soul or spirit in its manner of being, that is, that just as the spirit has being, so does the body, this has already been refuted in the previous argument. For, if this being has no attributes or perfections like those of spirit, then this is a mere fiction. For God has created no bare being, which is only mere being and without attributes, which can be predicated of it. Moreover, being is merely a logical term and concept, which logicians call the most general genus and which, as a bare and abstract notion, does not exist in things themselves but only as a concept or in the human mind. For this reason, every being has an individual nature with certain ascertainable attributes.

Now, what are those attributes of the body which are similar to those of the spirit? Let us examine the principal attributes of the body insofar as it is distinct from the spirit. According to the sense of those who maintain that body and spirit are so infinitely distant in nature that one cannot become the other, the attributes are the following: that the body is impenetrable by all other bodies, so that their parts cannot penetrate each other. Another attribute of the body is that it is discerpible, or divisible. The attributes of spirit, however, as these people define them, are penetrability and indiscerpibility, so that one spirit can penetrate another or a thousand spirits can exist within each other, taking up no more space than one spirit. Moreover, spirit is so simple and unified that it cannot be separated or really divided into parts separated from each other. Now, if we compare these attributes of body and spirit, they are so far from having any similarity to each other or of having any natural affinity – yet the true basis of love and unity consists in this, as has been said – that they are clearly opposites. Indeed, nothing in the entire universe can be conceived of as so contrary, as body and spirit are in the minds of these people. For in all their attributes they are utterly contrary because impenetrability and penetrability are more opposite than black and white or hot and cold, since black can become white and hot can become cold. But, as they say, what is impenetrable cannot become penetrable. Yet God and creatures are not so infinitely different in their essence as these doctors make body and spirit, for there are many attributes which God and creatures share. But we can find no attribute of body which agrees in any way with spirit and, therefore, with God who is the highest and purest spirit. Therefore, body could not be one of God's creatures, but must be merely non-being or a fiction. Moreover, just as body and spirit have different attributes of impenetrability and penetrability, so they differ in terms of discerpibility and indiscerpibility.

But if they allege that body and spirit agree in certain attributes, such as extension, motion, and shape, with the result that spirit has extension and is able to reach from one place to another, move from one place to another, and also change itself into whatever shape it pleases, in such cases it agrees with the body and the body with it. To this I respond with my first supposition, that spirit can extend (which nevertheless many, in fact, most people deny, who claim that body and soul are essentially different). Yet the extension of spirit and body, as they understand it, differs in an astonishing way. For the extension of the body is always impenetrable. In fact, in respect to the body, to be extended and to be impenetrable are only one real attribute stated in terms of two mental and logical notions or ways of speaking. For what is extension unless the body is impenetrable, wherever it is, in its own parts? Remove this attribute of impenetrability from the body and it can no longer be conceived of as extended. Furthermore, according to the notion of those people, the extension of body and spirit differ infinitely. Whatever extension a body has is so necessary and essential to it that it is impossible for it to be extended more or less. However, according to these people, spirit can be extended more or less. And since mobility and the capacity for having a shape follow from extension – spirit has a far different shape and mobility than body because spirit is able to move and shape itself, which the body cannot do – by the same reasoning, what is valid against one attribute is valid also against the others.

S. 4. Moreover, how can they prove that impenetrability is an essential attribute of the body or penetrability an essential attribute of the spirit? Why can the body not be more or less impenetrable and spirit more or less penetrable, as can happen, and indeed does, with other attributes? For example, a certain body can be more or less heavy or light, dense or rare, solid or liquid, hot or cold. Therefore, why can it not also be more or less impenetrable and penetrable? If one says that we always see in these changes that the body remains impenetrable, just as iron when it is tempered remains impenetrable, I concede that it remains impenetrable by any other equally coarse body. But it can be penetrated and is penetrated by a more subtle body, namely, by fire, which enters it and penetrates all its parts. It thus becomes soft, and if the fire is strong, it completely liquefies. If against this they object that the fire does not enter the iron in a philosophical sense, as if the fire and the iron occupy only one place and are consequently most intimately present one to the other, since it is clearly not true that tempered iron swells and takes on greater mass than when cold, or that when cooled it becomes hard again and returns to its former dimensions. To this I reply that if they understand by penetration what we call intimate presence, as when a certain homogeneous substance enters into another of an equal size, which should not increase in size or weight, this appears altogether irrational, and it would be an utter impossibility and contradiction to endow creatures with such intimate presence. This belongs to God and Christ alone as creators, who possess the privilege of being intimately present in creatures. No creature can have such intimate presence in a fellow creature, because otherwise it would cease to be a creature and would obtain one of the incommunicable attributes of God and Christ, which is this intimate presence. This, I say, should be attributed primarily to God and secondly to Christ inasmuch as he is the mediator between God and creatures. And as Christ shares mutability and immutability and eternity and time, he can be said to share spirit and body and consequently place and extension. For his body is a different substance from the bodies of all other creatures. (Indeed, he is the beginning of them and closest to God.) Therefore, it can be truly said that he is intimately present in them, yet is not to be confounded with them.

But to suppose that one creature can be intimately present in another so that it mingles or unites with it in a most perfect way, while not adding to its weight or extension, confounds creatures and makes two or more into one. Indeed, this hypothesis would imply that the whole creation could be reduced to the smallest grain or particle of dust because any part might penetrate another without adding more extension. If it is said that this only proves that spirits can be reduced to a tiny space, but not bodies, because bodies are impenetrable, I reply that this is begging the question because they have not yet proved that body and spirit are different substances. Unless they are different, it would follow that one nature is no more penetrable than another, according to their opinion. It certainly appears reasonable that time is extended in such a way into its due measures and distinct lengths that it cannot exceed those limits and therefore cannot be intimately present in each – as, for example, the first day of the week cannot be present in the second, nor the first hour of the day in the second, nor the first minute of the hour in the second minute of the same hour, because it is the nature and essence of time to be successive and to have one part after another, although God is really and intimately present in all times and does not change. It cannot be said, however, of a creature that it exists in all or many times and does not change, since a creature always changes with time; for time is nothing but the motion or change of creatures from one condition or state to another. Just as this is the condition of time and of a creature in time, the same applies to place or to mass or quantity. For just as there is no time in God, so there is no mass or corporeal quantity. But in creatures there is both time and corporeal quantity because otherwise they would be either God or nothing, which is impossible. Therefore, as every creature has quantity, mass, or extension, it necessarily retains that attribute as something essential to it, just as the essence of time consists of many parts and these as parts of others and so on to infinity. Nevertheless, one can easily understand how a lesser time exists in a greater time through an example: so many minutes exist in an hour and so many hours in a day. Moreover, one hour immediately borders upon the next but cannot be present in it. This is the condition of creatures because of their mass and size. Indeed, one creature can touch another but not be present in all its parts, but a smaller body can be in a larger and a more subtle body in a grosser.

This is the penetration which more properly applies equally to bodies and souls; for example, when a less gross body is able to penetrate a more gross body. But two bodies of equal grossness cannot penetrate one another. The same thing may be said about spirits, which also have their own degrees of greater or lesser grossness and subtlety inasmuch as they have bodies. Nor is there any difference between body and spirit (if body is taken not in their sense, who maintain that it is merely a dead thing lacking life and the capacity for life, but in a proper sense, as an excellent creature of God, having life and sensation, which belong to it either actually or potentially), except that body is the grosser part and the spirit the more subtle. Thus the word "spirit" comes from air, which is the most subtle nature in the visible world. Spirit is better defined in the *Kabbala Denudata*[P] as the central nature, which has the ability to emit a luminous sphere and to enlarge and to shrink it, which appears to be the meaning of Aristotle's *entelechy*.[10] Matter is defined as a pure center or a point without a radius, which Aristotle understands as privation. From this we must conclude that the impenetrability of creatures must be limited to their centers. The Hebrew word *ruach*, which means spirit, also signifies air. And because air has such swift motion, all the swiftness of motion is attributed to the spirit which is in a moving body. When common people perceive no motion in bodies, they call them from ignorance dead bodies without spirit and life. But truly there is no body anywhere which does not have motion and consequently life or spirit.

[P] *Kabbala Denudata*, ii, last tract, p. 613.

[10] An *entelechy* is the "form" of a body, or the force intrinsic and specific to an individual entity which makes it what it is.

Therefore, every creature has its own due weight or extension, which it cannot exceed and which cannot be diminished.

This does not stop us from seeing how a very small body can be extended into a space a thousand times larger than it had, as gunpowder when ignited expands miraculously. For all this extension occurs through the division of parts into ever smaller and smaller parts, which do not truly fill the whole space as great as it seems since every part has no greater or lesser extension than it had before. One must conclude from this that all created spirits, which are present in bodies, are either in the pores of those bodies or in certain concavities, such as moles make in earth; or else the created spirits make the bodies swell and acquire greater extension, as when fire enters into iron and makes it swell and stretch notably. Although this swelling of bodies cannot always be observed by our external senses, it cannot however be denied. For it is possible that a body can increase notably in its dimensions and become greater, and yet this increase escapes all external observation. In fact, it may be so subtle that it cannot be expressed in numbers. For example, let us imagine a body whose volume contains 64 parts and another of 100 parts. The root of the first body, whose cube is 64, is 4, so the side of that body contains 4 equal lengths. But the side or root of the other body, whose cube is 100, cannot be expressed as a number, for it is greater than 4 and less than 5 and no fraction can determine it. Bodies, therefore, as said above, can swell notably, if many spirits or more subtle bodies enter into them, even though our crass senses judge that they have not become larger.

Now let us turn to the second attribute which is said to belong to a body but not to a spirit, namely, divisibility. If they understand by this that one body, even the smallest conceivable (if we can conceive of such a body) can be divided, this is plainly impossible, for it is a contradiction in terms and implies that the smallest creature may be divided into smaller parts. Thus if a body is understood as one single individual, then it is indivisible. What we commonly mean by the divisibility of bodies is that we can divide one body from another by placing a third between them. In this sense, spirits are no less divisible than bodies. For although one single spirit cannot become two or more spirits, nevertheless, a number of spirits coexisting in one body can be separated from each other as easily as bodies can. However, in whatever way bodies or spirits may be divided or separated from each other throughout the universe, they always remain united in this separation since the whole creation is always just one substance or entity, and there is no vacuum in it. Therefore how can anything be separated from itself, that is, from its own nature as it was originally, primordially, or in its first being? There exists a general unity of all creatures one with another such that no one can be separated from his fellow creatures. There also exists a more special and peculiar unity among the parts of one species in particular. Thus when a body is divided and its limbs are moved apart a certain distance, as long as the limbs remain uncorrupted and unchanged to another species, they always send out subtle particles to each other and to any body which these particles reach; and that body emits similar particles (which we call spirits and bodies, or spirits, for they are both). Through their mediation, the limbs and parts so apparently separated always retain a certain real unity and sympathy, as many examples show, especially the following two. The first is this: if someone without a nose has a nose made for him from the flesh of another man and it is fastened to him like a twig grafted to the trunk of the tree in which it is inserted, when that other man dies and his body rots, that nose also rots and falls from the body of the living man.[11] The second example is of a man whose leg is amputated. When a surgeon amputates the leg and moves it a considerable distance away from the body, the man is overcome by pain and feels it in that part of the leg which was severed. This clearly proves that there is a certain union of parts, even when separated a certain distance from each other. Likewise individuals of the same species, or which have an affinity in some species, have a special unity among each other, even though they are distant from each other. This is even more evident in the case of human beings. For if two people love each other very much, they are so closely united by this love that no distance can divide or separate them, for they are present to each other in spirit and a continual flux or emanation of spirit passes from one to the other, by means of which they are united and tied together as if by ropes. Thus, whatever someone loves – whether it is a human being, an animal, a tree, silver, gold – is united with him, and his spirit goes out into it. It should be noted here that although the spirit of man is commonly said to be one single thing, yet this spirit is composed of many spirits, indeed, countless ones; as the body is composed of many bodies and has a certain order and government in all its parts, much more so is the spirit, which is a great army of spirits, in which there are distinct functions under one ruling spirit. It is now apparent that impenetrability and indivisibility are no more essential attributes of body than of spirit, because in one sense these attributes apply to both, and in another sense they apply to neither body nor spirit.

Against this infinity of spirits in every spirit and against this infinity of bodies in each body, one may oppose the following statement from Scripture: "God made all things by number, weight, and measure" (Wisdom 11: 20). Consequently a countless multitude of spirits cannot exist in one human being nor a countless multitude of bodies in one body. I respond, however, that this infinity or countless number of spirits and bodies must be understood only in relation to an intelligent creature, even though no intelligent creature can enumerate that infinity or measure the outward extension of a body or spirit which can occur inside it. It is freely granted, moreover, that God perfectly knows the number

---

[11] This is another example Lady Conway derived from van Helmont.

and measure of all created things. For if God made everything in number, measure, and weight, then every creature will have its number, measure, and weight; and consequently, we cannot say of any creature that it is only one single thing because it is a number, and number is a multitude. Truly, it is the nature of a creature that it cannot be merely singular if it has to act and enjoy that good which the Creator prepared for it. For example, let us suppose one atom separated from all fellow creatures. What can it do to perfect itself and become greater or better? What can it see or hear or taste or feel, either within or without? It cannot have internal motion because all motion has at least two ends or extremes, namely a beginning and an end. And since this atom is one thing, its center can certainly not have a motion from a beginning to an end; and since therefore it does not see, hear, taste, or feel within itself, it clearly cannot receive these from other creatures outside it. For if it were to see, hear, taste, or feel any other creature, it would have to receive an image of that other creature within itself, which it cannot do because it is only an atom and so small that it cannot receive anything inside itself. For just as the organs of the external senses are made up of many parts, so are the organs of the internal senses.

Consequently, all knowledge requires a variety or multitude of things as the subject or receptacle of that knowledge. Moreover, I understand all creaturely knowledge as knowledge received or aroused by the things or objects which are known (whereas God's knowledge is neither received nor aroused by creatures, but is innately in him and comes from him). Since there are various objects of our knowledge, and since every object sends us its own image and that image is a real entity, it follows that we have many images in us, all of which cannot be received in an atom, but they need their own distinct places in us for their distinct form and shape. Otherwise, not only would confusion follow but many things would be present one to another without any extension, which is against the nature of a creature. Moreover, although the objects of our knowledge are many and we know that I, for example, am a multiple being who receives many images from objects, it does not follow that if I am a multiple being who knows something, I should consequently see one object as if it were multiple, so that instead of one man I would see many. When many men see one man, they do not see him as many men but only as one. Thus, when I look at something, I see it with my two eyes (unless, perhaps, there is some defect in my vision), and two things do not appear to me, but one. And if I could see something with ten thousand eyes, just as I see with two, that thing, whether it be a horse or a man, would not appear as anything but one single thing. This seems to be the great difference between God and the creatures. For he is one, and this is his perfection, namely to have need of nothing outside himself. But a creature, because it needs the help of its fellow creatures, must be multiple in order to receive this help. For whatever receives something is nourished by it and thus becomes part of it. Therefore it is no longer one thing but many, and as many indeed as the things which it receives and even greater than that. Thus there is a certain mutuality between creatures in giving and receiving, through which one supports another so that one cannot live without the other. What creature in the entire universe can be found which does not need its fellow creatures? Certainly none. Consequently, every creature which has any life, sense, or motion must be multiple or numerous; indeed, from the perspective of every created intellect, it must be numerous without number or infinite. But if someone says, it is necessary that a central or ruling spirit be a single atom, for why else is it called a central or principal spirit having dominion over all the rest, I answer, no. For this central, ruling, or principal spirit is multiple, for the reasons stated above. It is called central because all the other spirits come together in it, just as lines from every part of the circumference meet in the center and go forth from this center. Indeed, the unity of spirits composing this central predominant spirit is firmer and more tenacious than that of other spirits, which are like angels or servants of the principal spirit and leader. This unity is so great that nothing can dissolve it (although the unity of the greater number of ministering spirits which do not belong to the center may be dissolved). Thus it happens that the soul of every human being will remain a whole soul for eternity and endure without end, so that it may receive proper rewards for its labor. The universal law of justice inscribed in everything requires this. This law is like a most strong and unbreakable bond in keeping this unity. For what can agree better with this infinite justice and wisdom than that those who agreed and united in doing good or bad will receive their reward or due punishment together, which cannot happen if they are separated from each other? For the same reason, the central spirit of all other creatures remains indissoluble. And although new central spirits are continually formed in the production of things, nevertheless no central spirit is dissolved; it can only be further advanced or diminished according to its current worthiness or unworthiness, capacity or incapacity.

Chapter VIII

S. 1. It is further proved by three additional proofs that spirit and body, insofar as they are creatures, do not essentially differ. And a fourth reason is taken from that intimate union or bond which exists between spirits and bodies. S. 2. If the way in which the soul moves the body is illustrated by the way that God moves creatures, this comparison is altogether false. S. 3. The union and sympathy of soul and body can be easily demonstrated, as can the way in which the soul moves the body, from the above mentioned principle that spirit is body and body spirit. S. 4. A fifth argument is taken from earth and water, which continually produce various kinds of animals from rotting and corrupt matter. S. 5. How gross matter is changed into spirit and becomes, as it were, the mother of spirits. An example is drawn from our corporeal nourishment, which through various transmutations in the body is changed into animal spirits and from these into more subtle and spiritual spirits. S. 6. Concerning the good and bad angels of men, which are properly human angels, and which proceed from him just like branches from roots. S. 7. The sixth and last argument is taken from some passages of Scripture.

S. 1. The fourth argument, to prove that spirit and body do not differ in essence but in degree, I take from that intimate union or bond which exists between spirits and bodies, by means of which spirits have dominion over bodies with which they are united, so that they move them from one place to another and use them as instruments in their various operations. For if spirit and body are so opposed to each other that while spirit is alive or a living and perceiving substance, body is merely a dead mass, and if spirit is penetrable and indivisible, while body is impenetrable and divisible – all of which are opposing attributes – then what, I ask, is it that unites and joins them so much? Or what are those chains or ties which hold them so firmly together and for such a length of time? Furthermore, when a spirit or soul has been separated from a body, so that the spirit no longer rules over it or has power to move it as before, what is the cause of this separation? If one says that the vital affinity of the soul for the body is the cause of this union and that this vital affinity ceases with the corruption of the body, I answer that one must first ask in what this vital affinity consists? For if they cannot tell us in what this affinity consists, they are talking foolishly with inane words which have sound but not sense. For, surely, according to the sense in which they take body and spirit, there is no affinity whatsoever. For body is always dead matter lacking life and perception, no less when spirit is in it than when spirit leaves it. Thus there is no affinity at all between them. But if some affinity does exist, it would clearly remain the same whether the body is whole or corrupt. If they deny this because spirit requires an organized body to perform the vital actions of the external senses and to move the body and transfer it from place to place, which organization is lacking in a corrupt body, this does not solve the difficulty. For why does spirit require such an organized body? For example, why does the spirit require a corporeal eye so wonderfully formed and organized that I may see through it? Why does spirit need corporeal vision so that it may see corporeal objects? And why is it necessary for the image of an object to be transmitted through the eye so the soul may see it? If it were altogether spirit and in no way body, why does it need such different corporeal organs, which differ from its nature so greatly? Furthermore, how can a spirit move its body or any of its members if the spirit (as they affirm) is of such a nature that no part of its body may resist in any way, as one body usually resists another when, as a result of its impenetrability, it is moved by it? For if spirit so easily penetrates every body, why, when it moves from place to place, does it not leave the body behind since it can so easily pass through it without any or the least resistance? Clearly, this is the cause of all those motions which we see in the world when one thing moves another, namely that the two are impenetrable, in the sense already explained. For were it not for this impenetrability, one creature could scarcely move another because they would not oppose or resist each other in any way. We have an example of this in the sails of ships by means of which the wind drives the ship – and all the more strongly the fewer the openings, holes, and passages there are in the sails. On the contrary, if instead of sails, a net were unfurled through which the wind would pass freely, the ship would barely move, even though a great storm was blowing. Thus we see how this impenetrability causes the existence of this motion and produces it. Moreover, if there were no impenetrability, as in the case of body and spirit, then there could be no resistance, and consequently spirit could not cause any motion of a body.

S. 2. If they object that God,·who is completely incorporeal and intimately present in all bodies, nevertheless moves whatever bodies he pleases and that he is the prime mover of all things, yet has nothing impenetrable about him, I answer that this motion by which God moves a body is completely different from the way a soul moves a body. For the will of God, which gave being to bodies, also gave them motion. Hence motion itself comes from God, through whose will all motion occurs. For, just as a creature cannot give being to itself, so it cannot move itself. But in him and through him we move, live, and have our being (Acts 17: 28). Therefore motion and being come from the same cause, God the creator, who nevertheless remains unmoved himself and does not go from place to place since he is equally present everywhere and bestows motion on creatures. But it is a very different case when the soul moves the body, for the soul is not the author of motion but merely limits it to this or that particular thing. And the soul itself moves together with the body from place to place, and if the body is imprisoned or bound with chains, the soul cannot depart from the prison or chains. If anyone wishes to illustrate the motion of the body produced by the soul through the example of God moving his creatures, the comparison is very inappropriate; indeed, they are as dissimilar as if someone wished to describe how an architect builds a ship or house by giving the example of God creating the first substance or matter. In this case the dissimilarity is clearly great. For God gave being to creatures, but a carpenter does not give being to the wood from which he builds a ship.

Indeed, no one thinks that because I say that the motions of every creature come from God that he is or could therefore be the author or cause of sin, for although the power to move comes from God, yet sin in no way comes from God but from the creature which has abused this power and directed it to something other than it should. Thus sin is ataxia, or a disorderly direction of motion or the power of moving from its appropriate place or state to another. If, for example, a ship is moved by wind but is steered by a helmsman so that it goes from this or that place, then the helmsman is neither the author nor cause of the wind; but the wind blowing, he makes either a good or bad use of it. When he guides the ship to its destination, he is praised, but when he grounds it on the shoals and suffers shipwreck, then he is blamed and deemed worthy of punishment.

Furthermore, why does the spirit or soul suffer so with bodily pain? For if when united to the body it has no corporeality or bodily nature, why is it wounded or grieved when the body is wounded, whose nature is so different? For since the soul can so easily penetrate the body, how can any corporeal thing hurt it? If one says that only the body feels pain but not the soul, this contradicts the principle of those who affirm that the body has no life or perception. But if one admits that the soul is of one nature and substance with the body, although it surpasses the body by many degrees of life and spirituality, just as it does in swiftness and penetrability and various other perfections, then all the above mentioned difficulties vanish; and one may easily understand how the soul and body are united together and how the soul moves the body and suffers with it and through it.[q]

[q] That this is the opinion of the Hebrews appears from a passage in the *Kabbala Denudata*, i, pt. 3, Dissertio 8, ch. 13, pp. 171 ff.

S. 3. We may easily understand how one body is united with another by that true affinity which one has for another in its nature. Thus the most subtle and spiritual body can be united with a very gross and dense body by means of certain mediating bodies, which share the subtlety and crassness in various degrees between the two extremes. These median bodies are truly the ties or links through which such a subtle and spiritual soul is connected to so crass a body. The union is broken when these mediating spirits are absent or cease.[12] From this basic principle, we easily understand how the soul moves the body just as one subtle body is able to move another crass and dense one. And since the body itself is sentient life or perceiving substance, it is no less easily understood how one body can wound or bring pain or pleasure to another body, because things of one or of a similar nature can easily affect each other. And this argument can be used to answer similar difficulties, namely, how spirits move other spirits, and how spirits contend or struggle with other spirits, and also how good spirits promote unity, harmony, and friendship with each other. For if all spirits can be intimately present within each other, how can they contend or struggle about their location and how can one expel another? And yet a few people who know their own hearts have learned from experience that there is such an expulsion and struggle of spirits, especially of good spirits against evil ones.

But if one says that the spirit of God and Christ is intimately present in all things and that it wages war and contends against the devil and his spirits in the human heart, I answer that this comparison is invalid when the operations of God and his creatures are compared. For God's ways are infinitely superior to ours. Nevertheless, one valid objection remains. For when the spirits of God and Christ struggle against the devil and the evil spirits in the human heart, they unite with certain good spirits whom they sanctify and prepare for this union and which serve as a vehicle or chariot in their struggle and conflict with wicked spirits. And so far as these evil spirits struggle against those good spirits in the human heart, they struggle against God and Christ. These good spirits are the spirits of that pious and faithful person who was made good even though he was wicked before. God and Christ help every pious person in this struggle so that they may prevail over evil spirits; however, God allows those who are evil and unfaithful to be captured and vanquished by evil spirits. For God helps no one who does not fear and love him, and who does not obey him and believe in his power, goodness, and truth. When he unites with these people, then the good spirits of such men are like so many arrows and swords which wound and drive back those dark and impure spirits.

---

12 That there were innumerable spirits of differing degrees of density linking body and spirit was a standard aspect of Renaissance philosophy. John Donne presents this in "The Extasie," ll. 61–4:

> As our blood labours to beget
> Spirits, as like soules as it can,
> Because such fingers need to knit
> That subtile knot, which makes us man.

If one asks, how can the human soul, even in the highest state of purity, be united with God, since God is pure spirit, whereas the soul, though pure in the highest degree, always partakes of corporeality? I answer that this happens through Jesus Christ, who is the true and appropriate medium between the two. Christ and the soul can be united without any other medium because of their great affinity and likeness, which those learned men cannot demonstrate who say that the nature of body and spirit are completely contrary to each other.

S. 4. I take the fifth argument from what we observe in all visible bodies such as earth, water, stones, wood, etc. What an abundance of spirits are in all these things! For earth and water continually produce animals, as they did in the beginning. Hence a pool full of water produces fish, although there were no fish put there to propagate. Since all other things come from earth and water originally, it necessarily follows that the spirits of all animals are in the water. For this reason Genesis says that the spirit of God hovered over the face of the waters, so that from the waters he would bring forth whatever was created afterwards.

One might say that this argument does not prove that all spirits are bodies, but only that all bodies have in themselves the spirits of all animals; hence every body has a spirit in it, and although spirit and body are united, they always remain different from each other in their natures and cannot therefore be changed into each other. I reply, however, that if every body, even the smallest, has in itself the spirits of all animals and other things, just as matter is said to have all forms within itself, does a body have all these spirits in it actually or only potentially? If actually, how is it possible that so many spirits essentially different from the body can actually exist in these different essences in a small body (even in the smallest conceivable) unless by intimate presence, which cannot be communicated to any creature, as proved above? Furthermore, if all kinds of spirit exist in any body, even the smallest, how does it happen that such an animal is produced from this body and not from another? Indeed, how does it happen that all kinds of animals are not immediately produced from one and the same body? This is contrary to experience, for we see that in all its operations nature has its order according to which one animal is formed from another and one species proceeds from another, either ascending to a higher perfection or descending to a lower state. But if one says that all spirits are contained in every body in their different essences, not actually but only potentially, then one must concede that the body and all those spirits are the same; that is, that body can be changed into them, as when we say that wood is potentially fire (that is, is changeable into it) and water potentially air (that is, is changeable into it), etc.

Yet if spirits and bodies are so inseparably united to each other that no body can be without spirit, indeed without many spirits, this is surely a weighty argument that they are of one original nature and substance. Otherwise, we could not comprehend why they would not finally separate from each other in various and startling dissolutions and separations, as we see when subtle matter separates from grosser matter.

How, finally, does it happen that when a body putrefies, other species are generated from this putrefaction? Thus animals come forth from putrefying water or earth. Even rocks, when they putrefy, turn into animals. Thus mud or other putrefying matter generates animals, all of which have spirits. How does the corruption or dissolution of the body lead to the new generation of animals? If one should say that the spirits of these animals are, as it were, released from their chains and set free by this dissolution, and they then form and shape new bodies for themselves from the aforesaid matter by means of their plastic natures,[13] I reply, how did the first body hold those spirits captive to such a degree? Was it because it was so hard and dense? From this it follows that those spirits are nothing but subtle bodies because the hardness and denseness of the body could imprison them so that they could not escape. For, if spirit could as easily penetrate the hardest body as the softest and most fluid, it could as easily go from one to the other without need of putrefaction or death to generate new life. This captivity of spirits in certain hard bodies, and their liberation when the bodies become soft, offers a clear argument that spirit and body are of one original nature and substance, and that body is nothing but fixed and condensed spirit, and spirit nothing but volatile body or body made subtle.

S. 5. Let it be noted here that in all hard bodies, such as stones (whether common or precious), and also in metals, herbs, trees, and animals, and in all human bodies, there exist many spirits which are as if imprisoned in gross bodies and united with them because they cannot flow out or fly away into other bodies until death or dissolution occurs. There are also many other very subtle spirits which continually emanate from them and which, because of their subtlety, cannot be contained by the hardness of the bodies in which they dwell; and these subtle spirits are productions or conjunctions of the grosser spirits detained in the body. For although these are detained therein, they are not idle in their prison since the body serves as their work place to make those more subtle spirits, which then emanate in colors, sounds, odors, tastes, and various other properties and powers. Therefore the gross body and the spirits contained in it are like the mother of the more subtle spirits, who take the place of children. For nature always works toward the greater perfection of subtlety and spirituality since this is the most natural property of every operation and motion. For all motion wears away and divides a thing and thus makes it subtle and spiritual. In the human body, for example, food and drink are first changed into chyle and then into blood, and afterwards into spirits, which are nothing

---

[13] As a dualist More needed these so-called "plastic natures" to bridge the gap between passive matter and active soul. Because Lady Conway accepted the monist view that matter and spirit were simply different aspects of one substance, she rejected this concept as superfluous and unnecessary. This rejection is further evidence of her independence of mind.

but blood brought to perfection. These spirits, whether good or bad, always advance to a greater subtlety or spirituality. Through those spirits which come from blood, we see, hear, smell, taste, touch, and feel, indeed, think, love, hate, and do everything we do. From these spirits also come the semen, through which the race propagates, and especially the human voice and speech, which is full of those good or bad spirits made and formed in the heart. As Christ taught: "The mouth speaks from a full heart and the good man produces good deeds from the good treasure of the heart" (Matthew 12: 34–5). Likewise, that which goes into a man does not defile him (Mark 7: 15), but that which proceeds from him returns to him in the same way it left him.

S. 6. And these are the proper angels of men or their ministering spirits (although there are other angels, both good and bad, which come to men) mentioned by Christ when he says of the little ones who believe in him, "Their angels look upon the face of my heavenly father" (Matthew 18: 10). These are the angels of believers who become like little children.

S. 7. I draw the sixth and final argument from certain texts of both the Old and the New Testament, which prove in clear and certain words that everything has life and is truly alive in some degree. As it is said in Acts 17: 25, "He gives life to all things," etc. In 1 Timothy 6: 13 it is said of God that "he makes everything live." Furthermore in Luke 20: 38 it is said, "He is not called the God of the dead but of the living" (although this applies primarily to human beings, it is nevertheless generally true of everything else). Certainly, he is the God of those things which have their resurrection and regeneration in their own species, just as human beings have theirs within their species. For the death of things is not their annihilation but a change from one kind or degree of life to another. For this reason the apostle proves the resurrection of the dead and illustrates it with the example of a grain of wheat which, having fallen to the ground, dies and rises again exceptionally fruitful (John 12: 24).

Chapter IX

S. 1. Philosophers of every sort have laid a poor foundation for their philosophy, and therefore the entire structure must collapse. S. 2. The philosophy treated here is not Cartesian. S. 3. Nor is it the false philosophy of Hobbes and Spinoza, but diametrically opposed to them. S. 4. Those who up to now have tried to refute Hobbes and Spinoza have allowed them too much leeway. S. 5. This philosophy is the most efficacious for refuting Hobbes and Spinoza, but by a different method. S. 6. I understand something else by body and matter than what Hobbes understood, and this has never occurred to either Hobbes or Spinoza except, perhaps, in a dream. S. 7. Life is as really and properly an attribute of body as is shape. S. 8. Shape and life are different but not opposing attributes of one thing. S. 9. Mechanical motion and action or perfection of life distinguish things.

S. 1. From what has just been said, and for various reasons offered that spirit and body were originally one and the same in the first substance, it plainly appears that the so-called philosophers who have taught otherwise, both ancient and modern, have generally erred and laid a poor foundation from the beginning; and thus their entire house and building is so weak and, indeed, so useless that the whole edifice must collapse in time. From such an absurd foundation, many other most crass and dangerous errors have arisen, not only in philosophy but also in theology with great injury to the human race, to the detriment of true piety, and in contempt of the most glorious name of God, as will easily appear both from what has already been said and from what will be said in this chapter.

S. 2. Let no one object that this philosophy is nothing but Cartesianism or Hobbesianism in a new guise. First, Cartesian philosophy claims that body is merely dead mass, which not only lacks life and perception of any kind but is also utterly incapable of either for all eternity. This great error must be imputed to all those who say that body and spirit are contrary things and unable to change into one another, thereby denying bodies all life and perception. This is completely contrary to the fundamentals of our philosophy. On this account it is so far from being Cartesianism in a new guise that it can more truly be called anti-Cartesianism because of its fundamental principles. Although it cannot be denied that Descartes taught many remarkable and ingenious things concerning the mechanical aspects of natural processes and about how all motions proceed according to regular mechanical laws, insofar as nature itself, that is, creation is very wise and has an intrinsic mechanical wisdom (given by God, who is the source of all wisdom) by means of which it functions. For truly in nature there are many operations that are far more than merely mechanical. Nature is not simply an organic body like a clock, which has no vital principle of motion in it; but it is a living body which has life and perception, which are much more exalted than a mere mechanism or a mechanical motion.

S. 3. Secondly, as for Hobbesianism, it is even more contrary to our philosophy than Cartesianism. For Descartes recognized that God is clearly an immaterial and incorporeal spirit, whereas Hobbes claims that God is material and corporeal, indeed, that he is nothing but matter and body. Thus he confounds God and creatures in their essences and denies that there is an essential difference between them. These and many other things are and have been called the worst consequences of the philosophy of Hobbes, to which one may add that of Spinoza. For he confounds God and creatures and makes one being of both, all of which is diametrically opposed to our philosophy.

S. 4. Yet the weak and false principles of those men who have dared to refute the so-called philosophy of Hobbes and Spinoza have conceded far too much to them and against themselves. Thus not only have they not effectively refuted their adversaries, but they have exposed themselves to ridicule and contempt.

Furthermore, if someone objects that our philosophy seems to be similar to that of Hobbes at least in this respect, that it maintains that all creatures were originally one substance from the lowest and most ignoble to the highest and most noble and from the smallest reptile, worm, and fly to the most glorious angel, indeed, from the finest grain of dust and sand to the most exalted of all creatures, and that it follows that every creature is material and corporeal, indeed, that matter and every body, and consequently their most noble actions, material and corporeal or flow from some corporeal design, I concede that all creatures from the lowest to the highest were originally one substance and consequently could convert and change from one nature to another. And although Hobbes says the same thing, nevertheless this is not at all prejudicial to the truth; nor are other parts of that philosophy necessarily Hobbesian, where Hobbes says something true.

S. 5. Moreover, far from being a help to him in his errors, nothing is as strong a refutation of his philosophy as this principle. For example, Hobbesians argue that all things are one because we see that all visible things can change into one another; that all visible things can change into invisible things, as when water becomes air and the greatest part of burning wood turns into something invisible, which is so subtle that it utterly escapes the observation of our senses. Thus invisible things become visible, for example, when water appears from air, etc. Hence Hobbes concludes that nothing is so lowly that it cannot reach the highest level.

In answer to this argument one may say that his adversaries generally deny the antecedent of that argument and affirm the contrary, namely that nothing of any sort can change into another. When wood is burned, many say that the wood is composed of two substances, matter and form, and that matter remains the same but the form of wood is destroyed or annihilated, and the new form of fire is produced in this material. Thus, according to them, there is a continual annihilation of real substances and a production of new ones in this world. This, however, is so foolish that many others deny that wood changes into fire and afterwards into smoke and ash. However, they still continue in the same error regarding other transmutations, for example, when wood turns into some animal, as we often see when living creatures are born from rotting wood or dung. Therefore they deny that wood has changed into an animal, for they say that wood is nothing but matter and that matter has no life or capacity for life or perception, and accordingly an animal which has life and perception must have its life from somewhere else and must have spirit or soul, which is not part of the body and does not come from it but is sent into it. If one asks them from where this spirit is sent or who sends it, and how a spirit of this sort and not another is sent there, they are in a quandary and open themselves up to their adversaries.

For a stronger refutation of Hobbes and Spinoza, our philosophy concedes the antecedent of that argument, namely that all kinds of creatures can be changed into one another. Thus the lowest becomes the highest and the highest (as it was in its original nature) the lowest, according to the pattern and order which the divine wisdom has arranged so that one change follows another in a fixed sequence. Hence A must first be changed into B before it can change into C, and must be changed into C before it can change into D, etc.

However, we deny the conclusion, namely that God and creatures are one substance. For there are transmutations of all creatures from one species to another, as from stone to earth, from earth to grass, from grass to sheep, from sheep to human flesh, from human flesh to the lowest spirits of man and from these to the noblest spirits; but this progression and ascension cannot reach God, who is the supreme Being and whose nature infinitely surpasses every creature, even one brought to the highest level. For the nature of God is immutable in every way and does not admit the slightest shadow of change. But it is the nature of a creature to be mutable.

S. 6. Second, when someone objects that according to this philosophy every creature is material and corporeal, indeed, is matter itself and body itself, as Hobbes teaches, I reply that by material and corporeal, or by matter and body, I mean something very different from Hobbes, and this did not occur to Hobbes or Descartes except in a dream. For what do they understand by matter and body, or what attributes do they ascribe to these? Obviously, nothing except the following: extension and impenetrability, which, however, are only a single attribute, insofar as mobility and the capacity to have a shape are reducible to the former. Let us imagine, however, that these attributes are distinct. It does not help or make us understand what this remarkable substance is, which they call body and matter. They do not go beyond the husk and shell, nor ever reach the kernel. They only touch the surface, never glimpsing the center. For they ignore the most noble attribute of that substance, which they call matter and body, and understand nothing about it.

If anyone asks what are these more excellent attributes, I reply that they are the following: spirit or life and light, by which I mean the capacity for every kind of feeling, perception, or knowledge, even love, all power and virtue, joy and fruition, which the noblest creatures have or can have, even the vilest and most contemptible. Indeed, dust and sand are capable of all these perfections through various successive transmutations which, according to the natural order of things, require long periods of time for their consummation, even though the absolute power of God, if he so pleases, may accelerate everything and accomplish them in a single moment. But this wisdom of God sees that it is more fitting for all things to proceed in their natural course and order, so that in this way they may achieve that maturity which he bestows on each and every being and so that creatures may have the opportunity to attain, through their own efforts, ever greater perfection as instruments of divine wisdom, goodness, and power, which operate in them and with them. For in this the creatures enjoy greater pleasure since they possess what they have as the fruits of their labor.

But this capacity to acquire the above mentioned perfections is an altogether different attribute from life and perception, and these are altogether different from extension and figure; thus vital action is clearly different from local or mechanical motion, although not separate or separable from it, inasmuch as it always uses this motion as its instrument, at least in all its dealings with other creatures.

S. 7. I have said that life and shape are different attributes of one substance. Just as one and the same body can change into shapes of every sort and just as a more perfect shape includes a less perfect shape, so, for the same reason, one and the same body can change from one degree of life to a more perfect one, which always includes the inferior. We have such an example in a triangular prism, which is the first figure of all solid rectilinear bodies into which a body can be changed. From this it may change into a cube, which is a more perfect figure and includes the prism. From the cube it can change into another more perfect figure, which comes nearer to a sphere, and from this into another which is even closer to perfection. Thus it ascends from a less perfect figure to another more perfect figure to infinity. For there are no limits; nor can it be said that this body cannot be changed into a more perfect figure. I mean that this body consists of straight lines on a plane, and it can always change into a more perfect figure. Nevertheless, it can never attain the perfection of a sphere, although it always comes closer to it. The same holds true for the various degrees of life, which have a beginning but no end. Thus a creature is capable of a further and more perfect degree of life, ever greater and greater to infinity, but it can never attain equality with God. For his infinity is always more perfect than a creature in its highest elevation, just as a sphere is the most perfect of all other figures, which no figure can approach.

S. 8. And thus shape and life are distinct but not incompatible attributes of one and the same substance. Shape serves the operations of life. As we see in the bodies of humans and brutes, the shape of the eye serves sight, the shape of the ear serves hearing, the shape of the mouth, teeth, lips, and tongue serves speech, the shape of the hands and fingers work, and the shape of the feet walking. And thus the shapes of all the other limbs have their use and contribute greatly to the vital operations which the spirits perform in those limbs. Indeed, the shape of the entire body is more suitable than any other shape that could exist or that could be made for the proper operation of human life. Consequently, shape and life coexist exceedingly well in one substance or body, where shape is the instrument of life, without which no vital operation could be performed.

S. 9. Likewise, local and mechanical motion, that is, the carrying of the body from one place to another, is a mode or operation distinct from the action or operation of life, although they are inseparable. Thus, vital action could hardly occur without any local motion because the latter is the instrument of the former. Hence the eye cannot see unless light enters into it. This motion excites vital action in the eye, which constitutes vision. And the same applies to all other vital operations in the entire body. But vital action is a far more noble and divine way of operating than local motion, and yet both come together in one substance and cooperate well with each other. For just as the eye receives light within from the external object which it sees, so it also sends out light or spirit to that object. In this light and spirit there is the vital action which unites object and sight.

Consequently, Hobbes and those of his party err gravely when they maintain that sense and perception are nothing but the mutual reaction of particular bodies, where "by reaction" he means nothing but some motion which is local or mechanical. For, truly, sense and perception are something far more noble and divine than any local or mechanical motion of any particles whatsoever. For vital motion or action occurs when one thing uses another as an instrument which serves to excite a vital action in the subject or percipient. And it can be transmitted like local motion through various bodies, although quite far apart, by which means they are united without any new movement of body or matter. For example, when an extremely long beam of wood is moved at one end from north to south, the other end must also move. This action takes place in the whole beam without any particles of matter being sent to provoke motion from one end to the other, since the beam is itself sufficient to transmit this motion. In the same way, vital action can proceed together with local motion from one thing to another when a fitting medium exists to transmit it, and this even at a great distance. Here one may observe a kind of divine spirituality or subtlety in every motion and in every action of life, which no created substance or body is capable of, namely through intimate presence. As shown above, no created substance is capable of this, and yet every motion and action whatsoever is. For motion or action is not a certain matter or substance but rather a mode of being. It is therefore intimately present in the subject itself, so that motion can pass from body to body even at a great distance if it finds an apt medium to transmit it. Consequently, the stronger the motion, the farther it can reach. Thus, when a stone is thrown into still water, it causes a motion which makes greater and greater circles from the center to the circumference for a great distance, in proportion to the strength of the motion, until it vanishes from our sight. Without doubt, it makes even more invisible circles over a longer period of time, which we cannot perceive because of the dullness of our senses. This motion is transmitted from the center to the circumference without any body or substance to carry this motion from the stone.

In the same way, external light, which is an action or motion arising from a luminous body, can be transmitted through water, glass, crystal, or any other diaphanous body from which it proceeds. I would not deny that a most plentiful subtle matter continually emanates from all luminous bodies. Thus the whole substance of a burning candle is consumed in such emanations, and the candle has that motion or action itself, which we call light. But this action or motion can be increased, for example, by a crystal when these subtle emanations of bodies may be compressed, so that they do not dissipate in such abundance that all the light passes through. But how can a crystal, which transmits light very easily, although it is hard and solid, receive so many bodies and transmit them through itself when other bodies, which are not as hard or solid, cannot do this? For wood is neither as hard nor as solid as crystal, and yet crystal is transparent, but not wood. Wood is certainly more porous than crystal because it is less solid. Consequently, light does not go through the pores of crystal but through its very substance. Nevertheless, the light does not adhere to it or cause some swelling but acts as a certain intimate presence since it is neither substance nor body but pure action or motion. In fact, crystal is a more suitable medium than wood for receiving the motion, which we call light, and hence light goes through one and not the other. Therefore, just as there is a great diversity of motions and operations of bodies, so every motion requires its own proper medium for transmission. It is therefore clear that motion can be transmitted through various bodies by a kind of penetration which is different from what any body or matter, however subtle, can accomplish, namely by its intimate presence. But if local or merely mechanical motion can do this, then vital action, which is a nobler kind of motion, can surpass it. And if it can penetrate the bodies through which it passes by means of its intimate presence, then it may be transmitted from one body to another in a single moment, in fact, in no time at all. I mean that the motion or action itself does not require the least time for transmission, although it is impossible that a body in which the motion is carried from place to place should not take some time, more or less great, depending on the kind of body it is and the vehemence of the motion which transfers it.

Thus we see how every motion and action, considered in the abstract, has a marvelous subtlety or spirituality in itself beyond all created substances whatsoever, such that neither time nor place can limit them. And yet motion and action are nothing but modes of created substances, like strength, power, and force, through which motion and action can be magnified beyond what the substance itself can do.

Thus we can distinguish between material and virtual extension, every creature having this dual extension. Material extension is that which matter, body, or substance itself has, but without any motion or action. This extension, properly speaking, is neither greater nor lesser since it always remains the same. Virtual extension is the motion or action which a creature has whether given immediately from God or received immediately from some fellow creature. That which it has immediately from God (from whom it also has its being) is natural to each creature and a proper consequence of its essence. In a stricter sense, motion is proper to a creature because it proceeds from its inner being. It is consequently called internal motion to distinguish it from external motion, which comes from something else and can in this respect be called foreign. When this external motion tries to move a body or some other thing to a place where it has no natural inclination, this motion is violent and unnatural, as when a stone is thrown up into the air, which unnatural and violent motion is clearly local and mechanical and in no way vital, because it does not proceed from the life of the thing so moved. But every motion which proceeds from the proper life and will of a creature is vital, and I call this the motion of life, which clearly is neither local nor mechanical like the other kind but has in itself life and vital power. This is the virtual extension of the creature, which is greater or lesser according to the kind or degree of life with which the creature is endowed. For when a creature attains a more noble kind or degree of life, it acquires greater power and ability to move itself and transmit its vital motions to the greatest distance.

But it is a matter of great debate how motion can be transmitted from one body to another since it is certainly neither a substance nor a body. If it is only a mode of the body, how can this motion pass properly from one body to another since the essence or being of a mode consists in this, namely, that it inheres or exists in its own body? The answer to this objection which seems to me best is this: that motion is not communicated from one body to another by local motion, because motion itself is not moved but instead moves the body in which it exists. And if motion were communicated by local motion, this motion would be communicated by another, and this again by yet another, and so on to infinity, which is absurd. Therefore the way motion is communicated is through real production or creation, so to speak. Just as God and Christ alone can create the substance of any thing, since no creature can create or give being to any substance, not even as an instrument, likewise a creature gives existence to motion or vital action, not from itself, but only in subordination to God as his instrument. In the same way motion in one creature can produce motion in another. And this is all that a creature can do to move itself or its fellow creature, namely as an instrument of God. Through these motions a new substance is not created but only new kinds of things, so that creatures are multiplied in their own kind, while one acts upon or moves another. And this is the entire work of the creature or creation as an instrument of God. But if it moves against his will, whose instrument it is, then it sins and is punished for it. But God is not the cause of sin, as stated above, because when a creature sins, it abuses that power which God granted it. Thus the creature is culpable and God is entirely free from every spot or stain.

If therefore we apply what has already been said about the attributes of the body, namely that it not only has quantity and shape but also life; and that it can be moved not only mechanically and locally but also vitally, and that it can transmit its vital actions wherever it wishes, provided it has a suitable medium; and that if it lacks this, it can extend itself through the subtle emanation of its parts, which then become the most fitting and appropriate medium for receiving and transmitting its vital action; then by these means it is easy to respond to all the arguments by which some people wish to prove that the body is altogether incapable of sense or perception. And it can be easily shown how the body gradually attains that perfection, so that it is not only capable of such perception and knowledge as brutes have, but of whatever perfection can befall any human being or angel. Thus, without taking refuge in some forced metaphor, we can understand the words of Christ, that "God can raise up children to Abraham from stones" (Matthew 3: 9). And if anyone should deny the omnipotence of God and his power to raise up the sons of Abraham from external stones, this surely would be the greatest presumption.

Index

Cambridge Texts in the History of Philosophy

Titles published in the series thus far

LaVergne, TN USA
23 December 2009
167918LV00004B/7/A